Managing Virtual Teams

Managing Virtual Teams

Second Edition

Debbie D. DuFrene and Carol M. Lehman

 BUSINESS EXPERT PRESS

Managing Virtual Teams, Second Edition

Copyright © Business Expert Press, LLC, 2016.

First published in 2011 by
Business Expert Press, LLC
222 East 46th Street, New York, NY 10017
www.businessexpertpress.com

ISBN-13: 978-1-63157-405-4 (paperback)
ISBN-13: 978-1-63157-406-1 (e-book)

Business Expert Press Corporate Communication Collection

Collection ISSN: 2156-8162 (print)
Collection ISSN: 2156-8170 (electronic)

Cover and interior design by Exeter Premedia Services Private Ltd., Chennai, India

First edition: 2011
Second edition: 2016

10 9 8 7 6 5 4 3 2 1

Printed in the United States of America.

Abstract

Virtual teams are an integral part of today's global business environment. Traditional face-to-face communication is frequently replaced with technology-mediated communication methods including phone, e-mail, fax, synchronous chat programs, and videoconferencing. While virtual teams offer various advantages to organizations and individuals in flexibility and the ability to overcome geographic distance, they face unique challenges. Virtual teams often are made up of members of various cultures and ages with diverse communication styles. Men and women also tend to behave differently in virtual environments. Challenges occur in the forming, storming, norming, performing, and adjourning phases of team development, and virtual teams must be able to cope effectively with those obstacles if they are to be successful and reach their potential. Team participants should be selected carefully for various personal characteristics that help ensure success and be trained in how to be effective virtual team members. Various team strategies can be implemented to improve effectiveness and satisfaction of virtual team members.

Keywords

distributed companies, team development, team strategies, technology-mediated communication, virtual teams

Contents

Introduction ix

Chapter 1   Growth in Popularity of Virtual Teams 1

Chapter 2   Diversity Challenges in Virtual Teams 11

Chapter 3   Strategies for Virtual Team Success 25

Chapter 4   Productive Virtual Team Meetings 49

Summary 61
Notes 63
References 67
Index 73

Introduction

A virtual team is a group of people that relies primarily or exclusively on electronic forms of communication to work together in accomplishing its goals. Other terms for virtual teams are *cyberteams, dispersed teams, distributed teams,* and *online teams.* A growing number of organizations are finding it relatively easy to employ readily available technologies to facilitate virtual team communication. In addition, virtual teams are the status quo in organizations that operate in a totally distributed fashion, with no physical home base.

Virtual teams play an important role in today's global business environment. In such teams, traditional face-to-face communication is at least partially replaced with technology-mediated communication methods including e-mail, fax, synchronous chat programs, phone, and videoconferencing. Most teams operate virtually at least some of the time, as members employ available technologies to supplement and at times take the place of face-to-face meetings.

It is no surprise that virtual teams have become enormously popular. For several decades, North American companies have employed teams as a way to respond to challenges associated with decreasing productivity, questionable product quality, and lagging worker motivation. Various economic and logistic advantages can result from the employment of virtual teams in organizations. But virtual teams also face various challenges, especially when the team includes members of different genders, widely distributed ages, and various cultures. Challenges occur in the progressive phases of team development, and virtual teams must be able to cope effectively with those obstacles if they are to be successful and reach their potential.

In this book, you will learn about numerous strategies you can employ to help assure effective functioning of a virtual team as well as personal characteristics you can cultivate in yourself and others to promote the development of valuable virtual team members and leaders. This second edition of *Managing Virtual Teams* also includes real-world cases with opportunities for you to reflect on how chapter principles apply in actual work environments, along with applications that allow you to hone your skills as a virtual communicator.

CHAPTER 1

Growth in Popularity of Virtual Teams

"More and more … work is becoming something you do, not a place you go." The workplace Woody Leonhard described in his 1995 book, The *Underground Guide to Telecommuting,* is quickly becoming the norm.[1] Leaders worldwide agree that virtual collaboration is critical for success in today's global business environment, and the likelihood that you will participate as part of a virtual team is almost certain. From 2005 to 2012, the incidence of telecommuting grew by nearly 80 percent, and nearly half of all U.S. companies currently use virtual teams. Of the more than 5,000 information workers surveyed in a recent study, 66 percent work remotely at least once per month and nearly one-half are involved at least weekly in virtual work.[2] Virtual work completed "anytime, anywhere" included that done by people who worked from home on a scheduled basis, those who worked on the road, and those who worked from home occasionally.[3]

Virtual teams, as defined by the Society for Human Resource Management, are groups of people who work across time, space, and organizational boundaries and who interact primarily through electronic communications. Not surprisingly, organizations with multinational operations are more than twice as likely to use virtual teams as compared with those having U.S.-based operations.[4] Virtual teamwork is critical to the success of organizations that establish and maintain strategic operations across the globe and that face a rapidly changing competitive environment. The implementation of virtual teams can minimize the inconvenience of bringing team members to a single location, cut costs, and attract scarce talent. As a result, many organizations are emptying their cubicles in favor of a virtual workplace that is radically different from that of just a few years ago. The following significant facts summarize the current trend toward the virtual workplace:[5]

- Of managers above the position of first-level supervisor, 70 percent now have at least one team member who is not colocated with them.
- In Fortune 100 companies, it is estimated that 70 percent of managers do not colocate with the majority of their teams.
- According to the Project Management Institute, the number of projects run by virtual teams has doubled since 2001, now accounting for over 80 percent of projects.

In today's complex organizations, having 50 percent or more of employees working on virtual teams is not uncommon. Currently, workers spend more than 80 percent of their time working collaboratively, often across 10 or more virtual teams.[6]

The power of information technology and the speed and reliability of communications networks have made it easier for organizations to organize, motivate, and manage remotely located employees. Managers report that the greatest successes that emerge from team interaction include brainstorming solutions for problems and issues, setting goals for team activity, and developing plans for team initiatives and projects. Various technologies are used to assist team members in sharing their wealth of knowledge and expertise and communicating with one another to find solutions.

Teams differ in their degree of "virtuality." Most face-to-face teams communicate virtually at times, and many virtual teams are not 100 percent virtual. Rather than involving a single type of interaction, virtual team communication can be achieved in several ways that generally fall into one of four categories:[7]

- **Same time, same place interactions.** These situations are similar to in-person interactions except that technology rather than face-to-face exchange is used to facilitate communication. An example is workers in the same office using chat or instant messaging to exchange ideas.
- **Same time, different place interactions.** Same time virtual interactions are known as synchronous communications. An example of a same time, different location interaction is

the use of texting between a worker in the home office and a colleague in a business meeting in another town.

- **Different time, same place interactions.** Various situations, such as different work schedules or lack of common time frames, can make it impossible or impractical for colleagues to communicate in real time. The time disparity can be overcome by communication methods such as a company blog that allows employees to share posts at their convenience.
- **Different time, different place interactions.** Different time interactions are referred to as asynchronous exchanges. These situations represent true distance communications. One method that works in such situations is the use of e-mail for communication between globally distributed colleagues.

Not so many years ago, the common view was that effective teams rarely had more than 20 members. However, a recent study of virtual team behavior at 15 multinational companies revealed that many complex tasks involve teams of 100 or more members. Research has also shown, however, that as the size of a team increases beyond about 20 members, the tendency to collaborate typically decreases.[8] As the number and size of teams increase, companies will clearly benefit from investing in virtual team development and training.

Advantages of Virtual Teams

Virtual teams have been made possible by advancing technologies. In today's global environment, work team members may never meet in person. Such teams are made up of people who are geographically dispersed to varying degrees and who communicate with the aid of technology. As international business activity increases, more and more work is done by virtual teams with culturally diverse members. Virtual teams offer definite benefits:

- **Cost savings.** Virtual teams offer flexibility and the ability to overcome geographic distance. Organizational expenses can be reduced when physical meetings are eliminated. Aside from the cost of airfare, accommodations, food, and car rentals, a significant cost of face-to-face meetings is associated with the time involvement of each expert. Travel time to meetings removes participants from productive activities they could otherwise be pursuing.

- **Labor pool enhancement.** People who could not participate in traditional settings can be part of the labor pool. Parents of young children, caregivers, and persons with various disabilities can be effective members of virtual teams. Virtual team participation also encourages appreciation of diversity through increased exposure to workers from various backgrounds and locations.

- **Facility and environmental benefits.** The need for office facilities and parking spaces is reduced when some workers are able to work from remote locations. Air pollution and traffic congestion are also reduced when fewer workers commute daily.

- **Employer efficiencies.** Virtual teams can increase efficiency by eliminating layers of management and valuable time lost to bureaucratic processes. Such teams also enable organizations to combine the specific talents of employees located in various places.

- **Employee efficiencies.** Worker satisfaction is increased due to greater flexibility in balancing work and personal life. Participation in virtual teams can raise worker satisfaction by helping people feel participative in shaping their own jobs.

- **Better decision making.** Virtual teams allow organizations to draw on a wide pool of talent distributed through the workforce. Teams offer a depth of expertise unavailable at the individual level and the opportunity for synergy of ideas.

Virtual Team Challenges

Despite all the inherent advantages, teams face real challenges that organizations must address if they are to succeed at going virtual. While technology can present its own set of problems, the commonly held view of experts is that virtual team success is due 10 percent to technology and

90 percent to people. Some challenges can be anticipated and mitigated before they occur, while others must be dealt with as they arise.

Lack of Nonverbal Cues

An obvious challenge inherent in some virtual communication methods is the lack of nonverbal cues such as facial expressions, gestures, and voice intonation. This void can complicate and confuse team member interactions. The use of audio and video technologies, such as webcams and Skype, can enrich the impersonal environment associated with text-only exchange. While synchronous exchange more closely mimics the face-to-face process of communicating, asynchronous methods allow participants to avoid interruptions and think more carefully about their responses.

Isolation

While some people enjoy the freedom of working in their pajamas, others experience loneliness and disconnection when working remotely. These workers can feel "socially unemployed" without others in close proximity to provide support and development and to manage their performance.[9] Camaraderie and meaningful relationships are harder to develop without in-person social exchanges that typically occur over shared meals, in informal hallway conversations, and in face-to-face meetings.

Lack of Cohesion

Virtual teams can lack cohesion, as relationships are harder to form in the sterile environment of cyberspace. The absence of actual physical contact makes interpersonal communication challenging, and the lack of nonverbal communication forces more dependence on words. The obvious objective of both face-to-face and virtual teams is to achieve their *task goal*—that is, successful attainment of their assigned outcome or challenge. However, to experience high performance and task achievement, teams must succeed in its *maintenance goal*—that is, the ability to get along and sustain long-term interaction. While not always recognized and articulated by the participants, the maintenance goal is critical to team survival. Team members must be able to maintain sufficient relationships with one another so they can work together effectively. If the maintenance goal is not achieved, the team will fall short of its task goal as well.

Cultural Complications

Cultural understanding is an obvious requirement for global collaboration. Culture affects the way people approach work, demonstrate commitment and collegiality, and establish expectations for effective teamwork. Obviously, the challenges of time zones and language are issues for virtual teams, as are varying views on leadership and business protocol. We will consider ways to deal with diversity challenges in more detail in Chapter 2.

Absence of Essential Behaviors

High-performing teams, regardless of their purpose, task, and mode of operation, exhibit common behaviors, which can be identified as the four Cs:[10]

- **Commitment.** Team members are committed to the mission, values, goals, and expectations of the team and the organization.
- **Cooperation.** Team members have a shared sense of purpose, mutual gain, and team processes and are willing to work together for the good of the team.
- **Communication.** Team members are able to communicate well with one another and with management. They are willing to confront problems and seek to resolve them in productive ways.
- **Contribution.** The work of the team is fairly distributed among members, with each contributing according to his or her expertise and experience.

The lack of any one of the four Cs will almost certainly spell failure for a team or, at the minimum, result in a less-than-optimal performance level. Research and reported experiences both indicate that the establishment of the four Cs is often more difficult in virtual teams than in face-to-face interactions. One reason is that virtual team members tend to share less information with one another initially, though disclosure typically does tend to expand over time.

Lack of Coordination

Coordination of work is more challenging in virtual teams, as team roles do not emerge as easily as in face-to-face situations. Needed task roles will vary with the assignment. Maintenance roles are also needed, such as members who serve as harmonizers when tension mounts, those who record and report, and those who help facilitate discussions and meeting progress. Effective leadership and efficient planning and communication are essential if a virtual team is to succeed.

Ineffective Leadership

Virtual teams require exceptional leadership. An effective virtual team leader must be able to skillfully leverage team talent, include all members, provide the team with clear work goals and other necessary information, promote trust, encourage healthy discussions and human interaction, and manage conflict. Successful teams frequently are characterized by distributed leadership, relying on various team members to take on leadership responsibility proactively as required.

You will explore these challenges and consider ways to deal with them as you progress through this book.

Case 1.1: AppendTo Seeks the Best and Brightest, No Matter Where They Live

While only a few years old, web development company appendTo lists its clients as including Celebrity Cruises, Time.com, Lenovo, Pearson, Purdue, Microsoft, and Blackberry. Although the company has a physical office in Hoffman Estates, Illinois, its operations occur remotely from around the country. The company's website describes the firm's operations as 100 percent distributed. From its beginning in 2009, appendTo's staffing philosophy was to hire the best and brightest, no matter where they live. In fact, the ability to work from anywhere is one of the company's core values. Staff members are encouraged to work from the locations that best foster individual creativity and productivity. While geographically dispersed, the staff engages regularly in chat conversation and other virtual shared experiences to stay connected to one another.

According to appendTo CEO Mike Hostetler, the key to making geographic dispersion a success has been the company's perspective of translating the normal human interactions they find in a physical office into the virtual environment.

> One of the simplest habits we train every employee on is the Office Door Effect. When you work in a physical office, depending on the layout, humans observe when others enter or exit the building. We replicate this by asking everyone to drop a message into a chat room when they arrive for work, when they leave, or when they briefly step away.

This practice leads to a chat room with many small comments such as "Good morning" or "Stepping away for a moment." The chat provides an easy and asynchronous way to discover where people are when they don't immediately respond to a chat message. Hostetler adds that the staff has a special "heads down" status that typically means someone is online for "emergency" purposes, but otherwise should not be disturbed while concentrating on a particular task or problem.

Virtual companies such as appendTo are finding that when people are comfortable in their personal environment, they are more productive and efficient in their job performance. Strategies can be devised to build a sense of community and sharing that might otherwise be lost in the virtual environment.[11]

Reflect

1. What unique challenges are faced by organizations with a highly distributed workforce?
2. How do virtual workers in your organization indicate presence and involvement?

Apply

1. Review the blog posts at appendTo.com. Compose a blog post for your organization that focuses on the advantages of a distributed workforce.
2. Read the following article about the company's success stories with virtual teams:[12]

Reynolds, B. W. (2015, March 30). 76 virtual companies and distributed teams. Retrieved from https://www.flexjobs.com/blog/post/76-virtual-companies-and-distributed-teams/

Select five of the featured companies and prepare a presentation on the common behaviors and strategies that lead to success in virtual environments.

Case 1.2: Johnson & Johnson Puts a Face on Virtual Team Members

Karan Sorensen, former chief information officer and vice president for information management for Johnson & Johnson's pharmaceutical research and development, understood the importance of uniting virtual teams and had firsthand experience in helping her teams overcome the cultural and psychological hurdles of remote electronic communications. She knew that one's cultural group has a significant impact on how the individual views his or her work and interaction with others in a work situation. Cultural differences occur not only among teams with wide geographic distribution but also in teams with diverse backgrounds and experiences. For example, occupational groups, such as engineering, purchasing, or marketing, also have their own cultures, and people carry these multiple identities with them when they join virtual teams.

During a global infrastructure project, Sorensen first brought her team together for a face-to-face meeting so everyone could get to know one another. Early on, the members set up rules of engagement—each person's preferred mode of communication and cultural expectations about leadership and status, appropriate work practices, communication with superiors and subordinates, meeting participation, the use of time and definition of what constitutes a deadline, quality, decision making, and problem solving. Call times were alternated so certain people were not always stuck dialing in at midnight.

Development of an e-mail etiquette guide helped everyone manage expectations, and during virtual meetings, the team referred to photos of their team members. A testament to Sorensen's leadership, the project came in under budget and ahead of schedule, saving Johnson & Johnson over $200 million over a three-year period.[13]

Reflect

1. What cultural and psychological hurdles would need to be cleared in your organization for effective virtual communication to occur?
2. How would you bring together team members in your organization who are culturally different?

Apply

Develop an e-mail etiquette guide for your organization's virtual teams.

CHAPTER 2

Diversity Challenges in Virtual Teams

As we discussed in Chapter 1, participation in virtual teams is an increasingly important phenomenon. The fact that technology makes connectivity and collaboration rather simple can lead to the mistaken assumption that people everywhere approach work in the same way. Diverse teams have the potential for greater conflict than teams in which members have similar background experiences and characteristics. Diversity can express itself in a variety of forms, including, age, gender, and culture, all of which impact the way individuals approach their work. While it can result in more creativity and greater problem-solving abilities, diversity can also complicate communication. Members of diverse teams often have communication styles that differ as well as varying ways of conveying information.

Age Differences

Age diversity is an obvious reality in the workplace, and the span increases as younger workers enter the workplace and as a greater number of older workers stay on the job longer. Fostering effective communication between four generations with an age difference of up to 60 years is especially challenging for companies committed to innovative teambased arrangements.

The following generations make up today's U.S. workforce.

- **Matures (also called seniors).** *Matures*, or *seniors* over 70 years of age, make up a minimal and declining proportion of the U.S. workforce that will continue to decrease to less than 1 percent by 2020. Their survival of hard times causes them to value hard work, sacrifice, and a strong sense of right and wrong. Many plan to reenter the job market in some capacity after retirement or stay there for the long haul.

- **Baby Boomers (also called Boomers).** *Boomers* account for less than 30 percent of the U.S. workforce and are referred to as the "me" generation because they grew up in the boom times following World War II and were indulged and encouraged by their parents to believe their opportunities were limitless. They will work longer than their parents because of better health, greater financial strain, and a limited retirement budget.

- **Generation Xers.** Generation X is proportionately small compared to the generation that precedes and follows it due to low birth rates during the inclusive period. Born in the 1960s and 1970s, the "latchkey" *Generation X* kids are fiercely independent, self-directed, and resourceful. As a whole, they are skeptical of authority and institutions because they entered the workforce in a time of downsizing and cutbacks. Xers account for about 34 percent of today's workforce.[1]

- **Generation Yers (also called Millennials).** Gen Y, the grandchildren of the Boomers, currently account for about 35 percent of the workforce. Gen Yers are technologically savvy, active, and globally oriented due to their lifetime experience in a high-tech world. They perceive work as a chance to develop their personal skills portfolios. Publicized corporate scandals have taught them to be more concerned about themselves than about their employers. In 2015, the Millennials became the largest sector of the U.S. workforce, and their numbers will continue to grow.[2]

- **Generation Z.** The next generation has been labeled Generation Z and is beginning its insurgence into the workforce. Times of uncertainty and war shaped Gen Z and differentiate them from their Gen Y predecessors. Gen Zers are even more tech savvy and socially connected than their Gen Y predecessors and are likely to bring strong collaboration skills and creativity to the job, though their social skills may be lacking.[3]

While individual differences exist, each generation is a product of the knowledge, experiences, and values that prevailed during their segment of history. Understanding and appreciating such factors can improve communication between people of various generations. Furthermore, studies indicate that concerns over generational conflict are often unfounded. For instance, Boomer resistance to Generation Xers might be based on an assumption that the casual attitude of members of the younger generation indicates they are slackers. Experience, however, has revealed Generation Xers' positive characteristics. Similarly, Gen Xers may look critically at the lack of responsibility, sloppy work habits, and crude manners exhibited by Gen Y and Z, and fail to recognize the value of the energy and enthusiasm these younger workers bring to the table.

When properly managed, companies with a strong mix of older and younger workers have a distinct competitive edge. Younger workers bring new ideas, a broad range of technology skills, and an eagerness to adopt new ideas, while older workers contribute a strong work ethic, experience, and institutional memory.

Encouraging team members who are quite diverse in age to work together requires effective communication, an appreciation for the value of diversity, and patience in learning new ways of interacting with people from vastly talented yet differing generations. Team members can enhance their generational competence in several ways:[4]

- **Learn about other generations.** Team members can gain valuable insights into other generations by reading excellent books such as *When Generations Collide,*[5] participating in diversity training, and beginning a mentoring relationship with someone of a different generation.
- **Become familiar with linguistic differences among generations.** Differences in language usage peculiar to some generations are a frequent cause of confusion and clashes. For example, the terms *freaked out, lame,* and *stoked* would likely mean different things to a 22-year-old than to a 65-year-old.
- **Be flexible and give people the benefit of the doubt.** Employees of different generations will thrive in environments where they are encouraged to learn from people of different

ages, not to become one another. Misunderstandings and confusion often occur because of lack of understanding or false assumptions. Seek to understand and ask questions rather than make quick judgments.

- **Don't forget the little things.** Not using appropriate greetings and closings in e-mail messages are little things that can be offensive to older, more traditional team members. Cultivating strong interpersonal relationships that enhance trust and open communication is especially important when dealing with an age-diverse workforce.

While knowledge of the characteristics of the various generations can be helpful in adjusting behavior and communication styles, team members should avoid the trap of stereotyping individuals according to their age. Effective team members seek to understand each person individually.

Gender Differences

Differences in the way men and women think affect the way people work in and manage remote teams. In *The Female Vision: Women's Real Power at Work*, Helgesen and Johnson cite research showing that women are highly skilled multitaskers, which can cause them to overcommit. Those who manage remote women workers can benefit from understanding that women's tendency to overcommit can lead to burnout and diminished creative thought. On the other hand, men's ability to focus on one thing for a long time can lead to tunnel vision and insensitivity to people and behavior not seen as "mission critical." While time on task can be perceived as yielding better results, often short bursts of concentration produce better outcomes than agonizing for longer periods.[6]

Another major gender difference affecting team management is the fact that women generally are more likely to speak up if they are unhappy with their immediate circumstances and environment, while men tend to suffer in silence and tolerate the situation much longer. Research on communication patterns in mixed-gender work groups shows that the traditional behaviors of men and women may restrict the richness of discussion and limit group productivity. The typical male approach to work tasks is confrontational and results oriented, whereas the female method of working is collaborative and oriented toward concern for individuals. The adversarial male style leads to respect, while the collaborative female style engenders rapport. Differences in male and female behavior that accentuate gender differences are often so subtle that group members may not be aware of what is happening.[7]

Until fairly recently, most research on the communication styles of men and women focused on face-to-face interactions. Current research has also addressed *computer-mediated communication* (CMC), such as communication that occurs via e-mail, instant messaging, and electronic meetings. Such studies validate gender differences in communication patterns. In one study, for example, women using CMC with other women developed more disclosure and a sense of community, whereas men using CMC with other men seemed to ignore the socioemotional aspects of group functioning and were more likely to use mild flaming (emotional language outbursts). Overall, men tend to be less satisfied with CMC experiences and show lower levels of group development than do women.[8] However, without daily contact and the familiarity of working in the same location, managers may experience difficulty in understanding gender-related issues in team behaviors.

Cultural Differences

Diverse teams frequently face cultural barriers, not the least of which are language barriers. Obviously, a certain degree of fluency in the common language used by the team is a prerequisite to effective communication. Avoidance of slang, jargon, and acronyms increases the likelihood that messages will be clearly understood by all. Beyond basic language considerations, however, team members must also recognize other challenges of cultural diversity and adapt their behavior accordingly. Recognition of cultural patterns and expectations and adaptations to spoken and written messages can improve cross-cultural virtual team interactions.

According to many team development experts, every team, whether face-to-face or virtual, advances through a series of predictable stages toward optimal performance. Psychologist Bruce Tuckman described the four stages in team development as forming, storming, norming, and

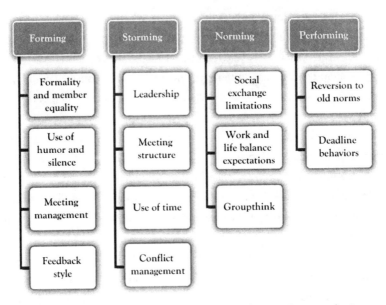

Figure 2.1 Challenges faced by cross-cultural virtual teams during stages of team development

performing. As culturally diverse teams move through these progressive stages of team development, various problems can arise, as summarized in Figure 2.1.[9]

Forming Stage Issues

In the *forming stage*, members get to know each other and to understand their team's tasks. In this initial stage, cultural expectations for formality influence the ease with which members get acquainted and interact with one another. Cultural differences will often be apparent in this initial stage and may play out in various ways:

- Members of some cultural groups—Asians and Latin Americans, for example—need to build personal relationships patiently before conducting serious business.[10]
- Ideas about equality of members can pose challenges to team development. For some cultural groups such as Germans, team members are considered hierarchically equal, while

for others, hierarchical structures play an important role, and subordinates are hesitant to speak out if a superior is on the team.[11]

- Issues can also arise from cultural differences in expectations for the appropriate use of humor, the use of silence, the way meetings should be organized and run, and how feedback should be offered.

Working relationships during the forming stage are typically guarded, cautious, and noncommittal—even in the best of circumstances. As team members size up one another in terms of strengths and commonalities, those who perceive themselves to be dissimilar from the rest of the group are likely to feel alienated and to lack commitment. At least one face-to-face meeting is crucial, as research indicates that when teams are unable to meet face-to-face—even once—they are less able to handle cultural differences and to understand and appreciate one another.

Storming Stage Issues

In the *storming stage* of team development, conflict occurs in interpersonal relationships. Interpersonal conflict resulting from cultural differences may be heightened because of different views on a variety of issues, including leadership, meeting structure, and use of time. Cultural differences during this phase of team development become especially obvious:

- The typical leadership style in some cultures (e.g., southern European) is relation centered, whereas in others (e.g., northern European), it is task centered.[12]
- Some cultural groups, such as Spaniards, are likely to feel that the leader should be followed even if differences of opinion exist,[13] whereas others, such as the British, expect consensus to be sought.
- In some cultural groups, such as the Japanese, preliminary meetings are preferred and expected prior to moving to the main formal meeting.[14]

- As in the United States, some cultures are more *monochronic* than others in their use of time, expecting exact times for meetings scheduled well ahead and specific start and stop times for meetings; lack of punctuality may be intolerable.

The manner in which those of various cultures handle conflict differs widely. Members of some cultures disdain conflict and often will not speak out when a difference of opinion arises. This approach can be viewed by others as aloofness, a lack of commitment, or even a passive boycott. Disruption can occur over different expectations for appropriate delivery of criticism. For example, Germans typically opt for direct delivery of criticism, while southern Europeans tend to prefer indirect levying of criticism. Austrians tend to prefer an approach somewhat in the middle of the two extremes. Some other potentially confrontational points for diverse groups include the following:[15]

- **The status of women.** Some cultural groups still hold to traditional roles for men and women, which may lead to difficulty in recognizing equality of male and female team members or the authority of a women leader.
- **Expected degree of politeness.** Asians, for example, find it appropriate to engage in small talk before getting down to business and may be put off by the "time is money" attitude typical among Americans.
- **Leadership styles.** The participative leadership style valued in the Netherlands is, for example, a weakness in Romania, where authoritative leadership is seen as a strength.

Norming Stage Issues

During the *norming stage*, team members find harmonious cohesiveness. Good feelings and the free exchange of ideas and feedback abound. Collaboration is achieved in the norming stage, though it typically takes longer to achieve in cross-cultural teams than in groups of people with similar cultural characteristics.[16] Points to consider about collaboration include the following:

- While greater friendliness typically occurs in the norming stage, some cultural groups tend to make a clear distinction between private and business spheres. Members of such cultures might be more comfortable keeping their interaction strictly business and avoiding casual conversation. Understandably, more socially driven members may perceive such behaviors to be snobbish or rude.
- For some, including Italians and Portuguese, having positive personal relationships with their team members is essential.[17] Extended social exchanges that might occur over a meal in face-to-face teams are played out online or via phone in virtual teams.

Managers and team members alike should be careful during the norming stage to assure that *groupthink* does not occur. Groupthink can happen when the team striving for unanimity refuses to realistically appraise alternative courses of action. The blinded thinking of such teams often leads to limited solutions and poor outcomes. Diverse teams are not as likely as homogenous, cookie-cutter teams to exhibit groupthink. But for diversity to promote the creative expression of ideas, individuals must be encouraged to apply their talents and experiences and to be open-minded to the ideas and views of others. Some members, such as is typical of the Japanese culture, will wait to be invited to voice their opinion. Silence might be interpreted as passive agreement by other members. The eloquent language of some members, such as the British, may be interpreted by some as agreement when in fact it is not.[18]

Performing Stage Issues

During the *performing stage*, the group becomes a truly collaborative team, with members inspired to go the extra mile to reach the team's objectives. During this phase, coordination of deadlines and meeting schedules is essential to success. Research bears out that when under pressure, team members tend to revert to their own culturally determined behaviors and ignore the team's norms.[19] Members of cultural groups who are accustomed to tight schedules will see those with a more relaxed view of time, such as Latin Americans, as idle and uncommitted. Some cultural groups are more willing to work through their private time, while for others working time and leisure time are starkly separated. Last-minute completion of tasks is easier for some to deal with than for others who prefer to work steadily and finish with time to spare.

Virtual teams do have a greater potential for conflict than do teams able to meet face-to-face, and cultural diversity that is often present in virtual teams poses additional communication complications. While variations in beliefs, behaviors, and expectations occur within all cultural groups, certain generalities about those from certain cultural groups can be useful for others seeking better understanding. Given little or no other information about an individual's values and behaviors, knowledge of the person's culture provides a good first impression of that person.[20] Experiences in cross-cultural interactions do serve to improve a person's abilities to adapt in similar future situations. Cross-cultural awareness benefits the team in several ways:

- **Overcoming stereotypes.** Experiences with those of other cultures are valuable in overcoming cultural stereotypes, which often stand in the way of effective communication. Gains from cultural exposure are not automatic, however, and require a genuine effort to actively observe, interpret, and respond to team members.
- **Mutual consideration.** Cross-cultural experience leads to the establishment of norms that support interaction among individuals and to the development of mutual understanding and consideration for others.
- **Language training.** Research indicates that individuals who learn a foreign language also typically gain understanding of culturally determined behavior and are thus better able to adapt to specific characteristics of the other culture.[21] The challenge of learning another language also promotes empathy for those of other cultures who struggle with understanding a new language and way of thinking.

Advantages derived from diversity are not automatic. To reach a high performance level, culturally diverse teams must work diligently to overcome barriers that could often be easily resolved in homogenous, face-to-face teams. The following suggestions can help you build cultural harmony:[22]

- *Select a skillful leader* who can perceive and facilitate handling of potential cultural misunderstandings.
- *Provide cross-cultural training* to team members to increase their ability to identify and cope with potential conflicts.
- *Strive for transparency* in all stages of activity, which aids in the development of trust. Set clear, specific objectives with no surprises that could be seen as hidden agendas.
- *Encourage the use of questions* to solicit input and check for understanding.

Tuckman, along with coauthor Mary Ann Jenson, refined the original team stages theory by adding a fifth stage called Adjourning, which is also referred to as Transforming or Mourning. Adjourning, is the dissolution of the group that ideally occurs once the task is completed successfully; everyone can move on to new things, feeling good about what has been achieved.[23] From an organizational perspective, recognition of and sensitivity to team members' vulnerabilities in this fifth stage is important, particularly if members of the group have been closely bonded and successful in their team activity. Managers in virtual environments must make the challenging decisions as to whether to keep particular teams intact for additional assignments or break them up and re-form for future work.

Understanding, appreciating, and addressing diversity challenges are important steps toward managing virtual teams. In Chapter 3, we will examine other strategic ways to promote team success.

Case 2.1: Sabre Builds Trust in Virtual Teams

Off the Mexican coast, with waves crashing around them, a team of five people struggles to keep a hand-assembled raft afloat. As the raft bounces uncontrollably, two people fall into the crashing waves. The remaining three rally together to pull their companions back on board. With all safely back on the raft, the tired team paddles onward.

While this scene may sound like a clip from an action-packed adventure movie, it's actually part of a team-building activity organized by Sabre, Inc. to develop its virtual workforce. Virtual teams make up a significant portion of the workforce at Sabre, a company that specializes in travel reservations. Distributed team members communicate via e-mail, phone, videoconferencing, and web-based conferencing. Sabre's teams are moderately but not completely virtual, with teams meeting face-to-face once a year and some team members working in the same location. The raft exercise is just one method Sabre uses to build trust among its members. Virtual team members at Sabre share some thoughts on other elements of trust building:

> When you are working with people you never see, you can develop trust, but you must respond to that person. Follow through. If you tell them you are going to get back to a customer, get back to them.

> You gain trust in people when all are contributing to the same idea and goal. You start trusting each other when you start meeting results and everybody has their role within the team and knows what their responsibility is and takes ownership to achieve results.[24]

Unlike face-to-face teams, for which trust results from social bonds formed through informal chats, impromptu meetings, or business lunches, virtual teams must find unique ways to promote trust building and build a base of trust on dependable performance. Sabre's leadership works proactively with virtual teams in creative ways to promote the trust-building process.

Reflect

1. Describe the characteristics of effective virtual team members. Which are the easiest ones to develop? Which require the most talent or effort to develop?
2. How do age, gender, and cultural diversity impact virtual team performance? What strategies can help minimize diversity challenges?

Apply

Design a trust-building activity that you believe would help promote trust in your virtual teams. Describe it in an internal blog post that motivates employees to want to take part.

Case 2.2: Promoting a Virtual Team Culture at Zapier

How can you go about building culture when there are thousands of miles between teammates? This important question is asked frequently by virtual companies such as Zapier, an information services company that specializes in connecting various sources of information into one integrated platform for its client companies. Zapier offers a variety of flexible work options for its full- and part-time employees spread across the United States and several other countries. "The first thing to realize is that your culture has to be built around more than ping pong tables," says Wade Foster, Zapier cofounder and CEO. "Games and other group activities that lend themselves to being in person are simply not a possibility on a day-to-day basis for remote teams. Therefore, your culture has to be built around something more than playing table tennis to unite the team."[25]

Just as a colocated office develops its own personality through inside jokes, shared experiences, and a collaborative environment, a remote team needs to develop something similar. Zapier employees use a variety of strategies to help build their virtual culture. *Slack* is the online version of the water cooler, where random work discussions happen and news, jokes, and pop culture are bantered back and forth. Discussions are recorded so nothing gets lost, and there's no "behind-your-back politics" that happens in many colocated offices. *Google Hangouts* is used for quick, *ad hoc* one-on-one meetings, and *GoToMeeting* works well for bigger team meetings. During chats, employees make frequent use of five-minute personal check-ups just to see what other members are up to. *Pair Buddies* is a weekly random pairing with someone on the team that allows colleagues to catch up on work issues and life in general. These activities keep some semblance of the office social life as part of work.

According to Foster, Zapier gets the whole staff together twice per year for a company retreat. During the retreat, employees take part in activities designed to help foster the organization's culture and build individual trust, including pairing up to cook team dinners and hiking as a group. "Getting things done tends to be a by-product of trust," says Foster. "Teams inherently evaluate each other on what was completed that week. We do this by sharing weekly updates on our internal blog every Friday—which creates a desire to finish something important each week."[26]

Reflect

1. What is your organization doing to promote trust and culture among its virtual team members? Is it effective?
2. How can performance be maximized in culturally diverse virtual teams in your organization?

Apply

Research one of the technology tools used by Zapier to promote effective collaboration. Compose a memo to upper management, describing the technology and explaining how it can improve the culture within your organization's virtual teams and ultimately increase productivity.

CHAPTER 3

Strategies for Virtual Team Success

Creating social relationships can be more challenging in virtual teams and take more time than in face-to-face settings. Virtual teamwork is not the preferred work mode for many, as people often feel isolated and detached from actual work production and from colleagues. Both leaders and team members require an understanding of virtual team dynamics as well as the possession of a unique skill set.

First-Year Team Strategies

Research has shown that virtual team performance typically peaks and then declines after the first year.[1] Unless teams can overcome early common challenges related to distance, technology, and coordination, members quickly face burnout. Various strategies have proven helpful in dealing with first-year challenges and laying the foundation for superior team performance.

Face-to-face contact. Face-to-face meetings, when possible, do help build team cohesion. Meeting together even once helps team members understand and appreciate one another, form cohesiveness, and tackle challenging group tasks with trust and a shared purpose. In situations where face-to-face meetings are not possible, videoconferencing, Skype chats, social media, blogs, wikis, and other collaborative aids can help provide the high-touch influence needed for continued success.

Clear team roles. A virtual team must take the time to define the roles of each member early and clearly. Assignments and responsibilities should be determined quickly with good record keeping for later reference. "Slow down to speed up" is a term used to refer to this important principle of virtual team development and change management.[2]

Review of communication strategies. Team members must review their communication strategies regularly to assess whether they are working effectively. Key questions to ask include the following:

- Is the time and frequency of meetings satisfactory?
- Is technological support for meetings adequate?
- Is the team using e-mail, instant messaging, message boards, or other channels effectively?
- Is every member's voice being heard?

Task accountability. Due dates and task expectations should be understood and accepted by all members with commitment by all to agreed-upon deadlines and conditions.

Performance monitoring. The team as a whole must regularly examine its progress toward the team's goals and adjust its strategy and individual assignments accordingly.

Leadership Selection

Selection of a qualified leader is paramount to virtual team success, and leaders who excel in face-to-face settings may not prove successful in the virtual environment. Virtual team leaders must not only understand the dynamics of team interaction but also adapt to the differences in face-to-face and virtual communication. Skilled leaders possess the essential qualities in Table 3.1.[3] Rate your own abilities in each category, with a score of 5 representing full competence.

While many organizations have found that the quality of output from virtual teams is comparable to that of face-to-face teams, more time is typically required for virtual teams to reach decisions. An effective virtual team leader must be skilled in moving people toward negotiation, consensus, and ultimate solutions.

Table 3.1 *Virtual leadership assessment*

Leadership attribute	Personal rating (1–5 points)
Leveraging team talent. You are skilled in selecting or making recommendations for team members who are a good fit for the project, as well as challenging each individual to maximize his or her commitment and contributions.	
Promoting a feeling of inclusion. You know how to make all members feel valuable and essential to the team's success. You expect and encourage all members to offer their opinions and input and recognize team members' contributions. You provide opportunities that allow team members to get to know each other and to build meaningful relationships.	
Providing necessary information in a timely manner. You are adept at determining what information is needed to get the job done and promote a feeling of engagement. You share information (formally and informally) in a way that allows team members to utilize it easily.	
Promoting trust and collaboration. You promote a change in attitude among participants from one of individual preservation to that of commitment to the team's purposes. You are able to guide the team in replacing initial feelings of anxiety, doubt, and frustration with a feeling of confidence in fellow team members and the team's ability to succeed.	
Encouraging healthy discussions. You are able to remain impartial and encourage sharing of dissenting opinions, as well as seeking information from outside the team when warranted.	
Managing conflict. You strive to reach consensus by encouraging discussion to continue until all members can say, "I am comfortable with that," or "I can live with that."	
Communicating orally and in writing using multiple media. You are able to express team goals and objectives and summarize the team's ideas and progress clearly, concisely, specifically, and unambiguously. You are comfortable using individual and group e-mail, online postings, phone, audio- and videoconferencing, social media, and other electronic means to disseminate information and provide feedback. You understand that regular, effective communication reduces feelings of isolation and disengagement.	
Demonstrating sensitivity. Through your words and actions, you show cultural awareness and sensitivity to different communication styles. You skillfully use knowledge of cultural differences to enhance team performance.	

(Continued)

Table 3.1 Virtual leadership assessment (Continued)

Leadership attribute	Personal rating (1–5 points)
Developing team processes that enhance commitment and accountability. You strive to delegate work, give team members freedom to make decisions, and monitor progress with structured, formal processes that allow for productive independent work as well as collaborative team efforts.	
Providing adequate resources to support the team. You ensure that team members have the resources they need to develop strong communication skills and participate successfully in virtual work.	

The collaboration of a virtual team with a wide range of expertise is required to solve many of the complex tasks businesses face today. Unlike the teams of years past, today's teams are often larger, more diverse, require long-distance cooperation, and include members with a wider range of expertise. An in-depth study of 15 multinational companies revealed that the same characteristics so important to solving complex business problems can also undermine the team's success. For instance, as the size of the team increases and teams become virtual, the tendency to collaborate naturally decreases. The greater the diversity of the team, including the number of strangers on the team, the less likely team members are to share knowledge or exhibit collaborative behaviors. The researchers found that the greater the proportion of experts on the team, the more likely it was to disintegrate into a nonproductive conflict or stalemate.[4]

To maximize the effectiveness of large, diverse teams, managers must take deliberate measures to promote collaboration. Best practices that help teams overcome the difficulties posed by size, long-distance communication, diversity, and specialization include the following:[5]

- **Executive support.** Teams do well when managers invest in supporting social relationships, demonstrating collaborative behavior themselves, and creating a "gift culture"—one in which employees experience interactions with leaders and colleagues as something valuable and generously offered.

- **Focused HR practices.** Team performance improves when the organization supports informal community building and provides training in collaborative skills. These skills include appreciating others, being able to engage in purposeful conversations, resolving conflicts productively and creatively, and managing programs. Some companies are finding success using virtual games such as "Warcraft" and "Ever Quest" to build leadership and team skills. The use of social media and blogs, wikis, and other online collaborative tools can help dissimilar people find common ground for communicating and sharing.[6]
- **Capable team leaders.** Assigning task- and relationship-oriented team leaders produces higher levels of collaborative behavior. An effective leadership style for virtual teams typically leans more heavily on task orientation at the outset of the project and then shifts toward a relationship orientation once the work is in full swing.
- **Team formation and structure.** Because team members are often reluctant to share knowledge with strangers, a best practice is to place at least a few people who know one another on the team. Cooperation increases when the roles of individual team members are clearly defined and well-understood, yet the team is given latitude on how to achieve the task.

Achieving collaboration requires a disciplined approach from the beginning of the project. The proper organizational climate, carefully trained virtual leaders and members, and clear team processes are critical to building collaborative behaviors needed to solve complex issues.

Virtual Team Membership

Working virtually has revolutionized the workplace, giving employees freedom to collaborate across continents while carrying their offices in the palms of their hands. While the vast majority of employees enjoy this newly acquired freedom, some individuals are better suited than are others for membership in virtual teams because of their temperament and experiences. Understanding the need to choose the right people for virtual work, companies such as Hewlett-Packard offer employees self-assessments to determine if they are cut out for the world of virtual work.[7] Careful team member selection is followed by intentional, continual training to develop lacking skills, continual effort to build strong team and leadership skills, and encouraging members to coach one another.

Strong technical skills are critical for virtual employees' success because collaboration with peers and team leaders separated by vast distances is most often accomplished through technology. However, managers are discovering that technology alone, even with the most dazzling gadgets and software, does not build teams. Instead, strong interpersonal skills are the secret to the success of highly effective virtual teams. This social skill set allows individuals to create a sense of community with far-flung team members so they can do their best work.[8]

Skilled members of virtual teams possess the essential qualities shown in Table 3.2.[9] Rate your own abilities in each category, with a score of 5 representing full competence.

Table 3.2 Virtual team member assessment

Characteristic	Personal rating (1–5 points)
Flexibility and adaptability. You are able to think about work in nontraditional ways and enjoy novel interactions with people of various backgrounds and areas of expertise.	
Strong communication and interpersonal skills. You can communicate clearly, concisely, and tactfully through phone, e-mail, videoconferencing, and so on. You are especially adept in human relations and able to reach out across technological barriers and cultural divisions. You understand that these skills are vital to your success because of the limitations on interpersonal communication inherent in virtual teams.	
Ability to think both locally and globally. You are able to grasp the immediate problem at hand and the broader implications of decisions, in terms of both organizational goals and team maintenance.	

Linguistic skills. You are fluent in the use of the dominant meeting language and know that being familiar with other languages is helpful.	
Listening (interpretive) skills. As a good listener, you are able to overcome distractions, focus, and reserve judgment until you have heard all viewpoints. You understand that while effective listening is important to all teams, it is especially critical in virtual situations devoid of nonverbal elements.	
Initiative and self-management. You are focused and highly disciplined, as much of your virtual work will occur without physical oversight. You recognize that being perceived as a competent, hard worker will help you build the trust needed to strengthen collaboration and free sharing of information when face-to-face contact is infrequent or impossible. You proactively take on leadership responsibility as required because you understand that successful teams regularly rely on leadership of team members as well as a dedicated team leader.	
Enthusiasm. To enhance team maintenance, you are an energetic, positive self-starter who inspires other members and regularly monitors your own level of engagement.	
Consensus-building skills. You know how to negotiate, mediate, and resolve conflict.	
Collaborative skills. You have learned how to collaborate effectively and work with others to achieve collective goals.	
Patience and empathy. You view your fellow team members as humans with limitations, challenges, and concerns. You are committed to helping make the team cohesive and enduring.	
Nonjudgmental attitude. You show tolerance for differences and appreciate diverse opinions.	
Cultural harmony. You are able to harmonize differences between cultures, genders, and ages so that healthy team activity can occur.	

Team Member Preparation

Virtual teams need competent and experienced team members to overcome the distance factor and deliver on the team assignment in a timely fashion. Team members should not only be carefully selected but also skillfully introduced to the virtual team experience. The following elements of team preparation will help ensure effective functioning:

- **Team scope and purpose.** These essential elements must be clearly understood by all team members. Creating a sense of importance helps to establish commitment and secure the "buy-in" necessary from each participant. This shared vision can be created early in the process by planning face-to-face or virtual team building activities focused on helping team members to get to know each other better personally and professionally and to establish principles for how the team will work.

- **Technological competence.** Comfortable use of technology is required for those who will communicate virtually. Unfortunately, technology tools are often underused in virtual teams due to lack of knowledge, coaching, and reward. Because virtual teams are so dependent on technology for communication, team participants must be aware of available information technology tools, know when to use each tool for maximum impact, and invest time and energy in needed training. Web meeting platforms, file-sharing tools, wikis, and other online tools can be used to create and share content and make important human connections. Assuring technical ability is probably the easiest aspect of preparing people to participate in a virtual team.

- **Face-to-face time.** Same location interchange, when possible, is enormously beneficial to virtual team formation. In addition to an initial face-to-face meeting for team members to meet and socialize, periodic in-person meetings are beneficial throughout the project life. These meetings help establish ties and strengthen responsibility to one another. Online civility and respect are enhanced when participants know each other beyond a mere online screen name.

- **Virtual presence.** When physical presence is impossible, strategies are needed to foster "virtual presence"—making a connection with the invisible virtual worker behind the e-mails. Without explicit efforts to create a "virtual water

cooler" where members gather to share information and rein-
force social bonds, meetings and other communication will
be merely task-focused. This sterile environment may limit
members' willingness to share important information and
weaken team cohesion.[10] Some companies encourage team
members to create team names and to use visual reminders of
their team members such as photos on their phones or computers. Using a company sponsored social networking hub or
Facebook or Twitter provides team members with a place to
talk about their families, vacations, and interests. Phone calls
and online chats allow virtual team members to share information about the whole person.[11]

Regular virtual team building activities should be planned to
strengthen connections; and if possible, the team should be brought
together periodically to relax and brainstorm important projects. While
strategies to increase virtual team happiness and productivity are critical
to build camaraderie and increase team cohesion, they must be designed
carefully to avoid overwhelming team members with more work.[12]

Trust Building

Trust is an essential element in all successful teams and is particularly
challenging in virtual teams in which members may have never met face-
to-face. Since traditional oversight based on constant scrutiny is impossible in a virtual environment, management of virtual organizations must
be based more on trust than control. The leader must set the example for
team trust and assist the team in developing trust in one another. The
following principles guide effective trust building.

The swift trust paradigm. The *swift trust paradigm* principle suggests
team members assume from the beginning that the other team members are trustworthy, and they adjust that assumption during the lifetime
of the team.[13] To achieve high trust levels in the early stages of group
life, virtual teams need social and enthusiastic communication. The team

leader should be positive about the team's purpose, effectively relate the importance of the team's tasks, and exercise skill in moving the team from social communication to task assignments.

Grounds for trust. Research indicates that high-performing virtual teams spend up to half their time in the first two weeks exchanging social information as a means of building initial trust, the first stage of trust development. As initial trust declines over time because of limited face time, virtual teams rely on cognitive trust, which is based on their experiences with each other. In this second phase of trust development, trust is earned by replying promptly and competently to e-mails, meeting deadlines, reliably attending virtual meetings, avoiding the temptation to multitask during virtual meetings, and following up on promises made.[14]

Team cohesion. Effort should be made to avoid putting teams together too quickly and pressing them to perform immediately without the luxury of important relationship-building communication. In situations that allow for face-to-face team time, trust-building activities can be used to enhance team member cohesion. Such experiences can range from physical ropes courses to interpersonal activities designed to promote openness, identification of common ground, and discovery of shared values and differences. By taking the time to highlight differences as well as similarities (cultures, procedures, time zones, and more), a virtual team can reduce the likelihood of judgmental behavior and increase respect and mutual understanding.[15]

Open and rich communication. Relying solely on online communication tends to inhibit trust, the sense of responsibility, and participation. Even if sophisticated technology is available, using richer forms of communication such as face-to-face contact helps sustain trust through long periods of online communication. In addition to e-mail contact, teams should consider establishing regular times when they can take phone calls or meet online to brainstorm or solve problems and remain online whenever possible for immediate and reliable access. This open communication can also facilitate resolution of conflict as soon as it appears.

Planning a Virtual Team's Initial Face-to-Face Meeting

The Galaxy virtual team has just been appointed and consists of six members geographically located throughout the United States. Anna, the project manager, has requested permission from management to bring the team together physically in one location for a kickoff meeting. How would you advise her on the following aspects of this first, and possibly only, face-to-face meeting of the Galaxy team?

1. The goal of the meeting:
2. The best venue for the meeting:
3. The agenda for the meeting:

Effective Communication

Maintaining effective communication in a widely dispersed team is essential to success. In fact, it is estimated that the time needed for planning for communication in a virtual team is at least double that required for a colocated team.[16] Team members can often have trouble getting in touch with one another, and frustration results when e-mails and phone calls go unanswered for days and individual progress is slowed or halted. Weeks can slip by without team progress as members are busy with their other job responsibilities. A lack of frequent and incidental communication also leads to mistakes that may not be identified until late in the process. Additionally, team members tend to have lower levels of commitment to team goals when communication is limited.

Studies of the communication practices of high-performing and low-performing teams underscore the importance of effective communication in the success of virtual teams. Studies indicate that high-performing teams communicate more than lower performing teams and with messages that focus on key aspects of the tasks. Researchers in one study concluded that the increased communication may have generated a greater number of high-quality and creative ideas. Leaders of the high-performing teams also sent considerably more and longer messages that focused on summarizing the team's work and sharing these summaries with team members. The summaries served a coordination function by keeping members aware of team members' ideas and progress. Many of the summary comments appeared in the final team report, providing evidence that the leader's summaries helped move the team from the idea generation phase to building consensus and generating the deliverable.[17] The following strategies have been shown to support good team communication.

Establish a Team Code of Conduct

Establishing a "code of conduct" at the team's onset establishes a commonly understood expectation for accountability. This clear, disciplined game plan helps alleviate pitfalls to optimal team performance. The code may include a principle of acknowledging a request for information within 24 or 48 hours. A complete response might require more time, but at least the person requesting the information knows that the request will be addressed. Keeping a common team calendar or having members post notices when they will be away keeps everyone informed about availability. The code of conduct might also address preferred ways for contacting team members, voicing opinions, and keeping time frames in mind for workers in different time zones. Expected behavior when participating in virtual meetings might also be addressed, such as not multitasking, limiting background noise and side conversations, talking clearly and at a reasonable pace, listening attentively, not dominating conversations, and so on.

Karan Sorensen, chief information officer and vice president for Johnson & Johnson's pharmaceutical research and development, set up rules of engagement for her virtual teams, such as identifying team members' communication preferences to address cultural differences, alternating call times so that certain members weren't always dialing in at midnight, and encouraging the team to place photos of one another by the phone.[18]

To be effective, the team code of conduct should be reviewed and adjustments made on a regular basis. During a virtual meeting, take the time to ask the following questions: Which agreements are working well and why? Which ones are not working? Do we need some new agreements or adjust some existing ones?[19]

Have a Regular Schedule of Contact

Since communication is the life-blood of a virtual team, scheduling regular contact with team members is vital, whether it is by phone, web, or in person. The leader may schedule a weekly videoconference and use e-mail or instant messaging for work updates or memos. Ideally, the videoconference should occur on the same day and time each week with a regular rotation of meeting time to accommodate team members working in different time zones with members. Leaders should share the meeting agenda in advance, enforce agreed-on communication protocols, and start and finish the meeting on time. Establishing and enforcing these rhythms in virtual team work allows team members working separately to stay connected to the normal rhythms of work life.[20]

Additionally research has shown that teams with a predictable rhythm of face-to-face virtual meetings outperform those who choose to meet "as needed" even if they have less face-to-face interaction overall.[21] Teleworkers in another study reported added stress caused by increased face-to-face communication, e-mail, instant messaging, and videoconferencing. Thus, managers must carefully weigh the value of any added communication.[22]

Manage Technology

Overcoming technological constraints is necessary for good communication. E-mail filters out the cues that humans give each other in social contact, thus reducing the richness of team communication, which can lead to less-than-sensitive communication and eventual team conflict. Deriving meaning from text alone can be difficult, especially when interpreting if the other person is expressing sarcasm or speaking tongue-in-cheek.

Emoticons (smiley and frowny faces and other visual depictions of emotions) offer a reasonable substitute for facial expression and other body-language cues. The following strategies can aid in overcoming technology constraints:

- **Choose an appropriate technology option.** With the message's purpose and human relations factors in mind, team members can determine when to reply with an e-mail rather than picking up the phone, take the time to create and post a document on a shared workspace, or schedule a virtual meeting. They understand that e-mail is not recommended for handling important discussions. Research reported by Kerry Patterson in *Crucial Conversations: Tools for Talking When Stakes Are High* indicated that 87 percent of those he managed admitted that using high-tech methods to resolve a workplace confrontation had not worked. Nearly 90 percent indicated that e-mail, text messaging, and voice mail can hinder workplace relationships.[23]
- **Use a good mix of synchronous and asynchronous communication tools.** This combination tends to produce the most favorable results. For example, a team that communicates solely by e-mail might save time but eventually face misunderstandings or a lack of team cohesion. Likewise, a leader who dislikes communicating virtually and saves all communication for weekly web meetings may overwhelm the team or not share enough vital information.[24]
- **Evaluate technology on the communication trifecta: simplicity, reliability, and accessibility.** Optimally, technology should allow teams members to get connected easily without complex setup time and steep learning curves, enable members to send messages to their intended target, and provide accessibility to the entire team regardless of location and time zone.[25] Collaborative technology must also archive messages for timely retrieval. These critical criteria must rank high when judging the merits of new versions of technology with countless new features.

Agree on E-mail Etiquette

When face-to-face communication isn't an option, a timely, well-written e-mail message can be key to getting work done, building trust, and fostering collaboration. The team might agree on an e-mail etiquette guide to enhance results and minimize communication that could be insensitive to different ages, genders, cultures, and so on. Remote workers may find the following e-mail practices especially useful:[26]

- Respond to e-mails at the beginning of the day, especially if working in different time zones, as many new messages may have arrived during the night or were sent out before the end of the working day.
- Give top priority to e-mails from the remote manager to provide assurance of individual and group performance.
- Reply "inline" to e-mails that contain numerous questions. Embedding comments within the questions will make the conversation easier to follow.
- Acknowledge a coworker's e-mail when additional time is needed to address the issue. A quick "I'll be in touch with you on Tuesday" will relieve the frustration caused by uncertainty and isolation.
- Be "present" via instant messenger or a web-based chat tool. Being available in this virtual space provides the same feeling as dropping in and out of a physical office to exchange short messages and files.
- Use the appropriate online collaborative tools for the task. For example, avoid sending file attachments back and forth when coediting a document. Instead, use a shared file space that allows for editing and then repost for others to access.

Craft Clear Online Messages

In addition to observing e-mail etiquette, the following advice will aid in creating e-mail messages that are read, have impact, and motivate people to take action:[27]

- Motivate the reader to open the message by including a clear subject line that conveys the message's purpose.
- Keep the reader's attention by designing a message that is visually appealing and easy to read. For example, use bullet points and boldface or italics to emphasize key points and ideas.
- Present the purpose of the message immediately and write concisely and clearly using short sentences and paragraphs. When scheduling a meeting, provide at least three dates and times from which readers can choose.
- Tailor the message to a single recipient rather than to many in the organization. Sending an e-mail to the right person will lead to results.

To avoid potential hurt feelings due to limited nonverbal cues present in e-mail, focus on being polite, keep the tone friendly and approachable, and avoid sarcasm and humor that could be misinterpreted by diverse team members. An intentionally positive tone is especially important when communicating negative ideas such as disagreement with another's opinion or idea. If possible, begin by sharing something that you do agree with; then, provide clear, supported rationale for disagreement and offer alternatives or suggestions that moves the discussion in a positive direction. Review word choice carefully, being certain that the language is positive and nonjudgmental.[28]

Use Phone Calls Effectively

With increased reliance on virtual teams, conference calls are taking the place of preferred face-to-face communication. Even routine conversations related to day-to-day work contain both verbal and nonverbal messages vital to effective communication. The understanding gathered from a person's tone, delivery, and body language is often more important than the meaning conveyed in a person's words, especially when the discussion involves an issue that needs to be discussed openly. Clearly, face-to-face meetings or at least videoconferences should be arranged for these important conversations so that both the visual and verbal data needed for understanding are available. While phone calls lack the visual dimension, the following tips can help you make them, especially calls involving conflict resolution, more productive:[29]

- Explain that while you would prefer holding the conversation face to face, you want to take special care to see that the problem can be resolved in a way that satisfies both of you.
- Take steps to ensure you are relaxed so you can maintain a conversation rather than starting off in debate mode. Breathe deeply, relax your grip on the phone, smile, and seek to understand what the other person has to offer.
- Pay close attention to what is said since you cannot see the person. Listen for pauses, tone, pacing, and vocal tension that would indicate the person is feeling stressed or threatened. Listen for words that indicate hedging or whitewashing.
- Summarize the conversation frequently and check for understanding since you can't see a confused look. Ask, "Did I explain that well, or should I take another pass at it?" Ask if the phone conversation is working to resolve the issue and make adjustments if necessary.
- After addressing a difference of opinion on the phone, follow up with e-mail to confirm understanding of what was discussed by phone.

Documentation and Evaluation

Effective virtual work requires deliberate efforts to document progress and assess consensus. The leader cannot take for granted that all team members are up to date on assignments and deadlines or that everyone is in agreement about the team's progress.

Thorough Documentation

Documenting team ideas, decisions, and follow-up is essential to virtual team success. Posting or sending team members copies of updated project schedules, completed documents, and schedule charts keeps everyone on the same page for discussions and facilitates individual work. Effective documentation also helps provide the transparency necessary to maintain cohesion and trust among team members.

The electronic environment facilitates the sharing of documents for current and future reference. For example, a "deliverables dashboard" visible to all team members on a collaborative hub provides timely status reports and tracks team members' commitments.[30] Traditional team documents such as agendas and minutes are essential for virtual meetings and are discussed in Chapter 4, along with other ideas for conducting effective meetings.

Checks for Understanding and Agreement

A prevalent issue in ongoing team success is the lack of project visibility. Team members often understand what they are doing individually but may not be sure how their pieces fit into the overall puzzle. Periodic assessment of team progress and member satisfaction will help uncover problem areas that need to be addressed. For instance, team members might be asked early in the team's development to rate the effectiveness of the team's meetings, using an instrument similar to the one shown in Table 3.3.

Virtual teams find it useful at certain key points in a project to take time to assess team progress and ensure any problems are out in the open. The Virtual Team Progress Assessment exercise can be completed as a group activity, with differences in opinion voiced and problem areas discussed.

Intercultural Training

Virtual communication can be difficult when it involves people from different areas of the world who have different communication styles. Low-context communicators, such as North Americans, who rely heavily on the meaning of words, are likely to find it difficult to communicate virtually with high-context communicators, such as Asians, who tend to deliver parts of their messages with silence or nonverbal signs. In such cases, the virtual method of communication, devoid of rich nonverbal cues, becomes an obstacle in itself.

Table 3.3 Virtual meeting evaluation

Attribute	Yes	No
Do I know the purpose of each meeting?		
Do I understand my role and the roles of other members?		
Am I prepared when I log on to meetings?		
During online meetings, do I multitask (e.g., check e-mail, read text messages)?		
Do I take phone calls or leave the group during online meetings?		
When I'm not sure about something, do I ask questions?		
Am I open to the ideas of others?		
Do I regularly participate in discussions?		
Do I stay on topic?		
Do I try to give constructive criticism to other members?		
Do I give high priority to logging on to team meetings?		
After a meeting, do I follow through on what the team has agreed on?		
If teammates cannot participate in an online meeting, do I fill them in about what was discussed?		
If I must miss an online meeting, do I notify other team members in advance and follow up with them for missed information?		

Intercultural training can help provide strategies and skills to communicate more effectively with international counterparts. Such training raises team members' awareness of potential differences in communication patterns and expectations and helps them find ways to both send and receive messages without confusion. Training is a perfect opportunity to bring the team together in a face-to-face context, or they can participate in a virtual training session to help them identify and deal with cultural challenges. Online cultural training is available from a variety of vendors and is designed to improve team skills and enable global team collaboration.

Virtual Team Progress Assessment

1. How would you rate the level of engagement of your team's members? Are all members contributing to conversations and projects? Attending and actively participating in meetings? Accepting responsibility readily rather than appearing overwhelmed? Working cooperatively with little unproductive conflict? Explain.
2. Are there team members who are doing an especially excellent job with coordinating meetings? Gathering data? Handling creative aspects of the project, and so on? Explain their special contributions.
3. Are there members who are *not* contributing what the majority of the group considers to be a "fair share"? Explain, including possible reasons (sickness, personal or family emergency, unusual work expectations, etc.).
4. What plans does the team have for allowing the low-contributing member to "make up" for the lack of participation?
5. Based on the overall performance and effort so far, what portion of the total possible 100 percent should each team member receive? You may divide the points equally or in any combination that equals 100.

Celebration of Team Accomplishments

Recognition of team accomplishments is difficult in virtual settings, as geography and expense often make physical celebrations impossible. Some teams are able to meet to celebrate in person at the completion of the project, but most must rely on "virtual partying." The team leader may offer group recognition for a job well done via e-mail or a conference call. While the team may not be able to physically take an afternoon or evening off from work to celebrate together, awarding members

Table 3.4 Virtual team leadership skills assessment

Team skill	Personal rating (1–5 points)
I possess the ability to establish a culture of accountability in which roles and expectations are clear.	
I exhibit zero tolerance for blaming others or finger pointing.	
I possess the ability to build an environment of trust among participants.	
I know how to encourage open and honest communication.	
I am committed to leading by example.	

with a free afternoon or day off following project completion is a tangible expression of appreciation and allows them to structure their own celebrations. The team leader can also use individual communications with team members to thank each one separately for his or her particular contribution and effort.

Manon DeFelice, founder and CEO of Inkwell, a specialized professional staffing company, often sends company-wide e-mails praising the team and singling out colleagues for notable work. She says these e-mails provide the same validation that an employee would receive if he or she were walking down the hall and the supervisor called out the praise so that colleagues could hear and know that this team member is working hard.[31]

Assess your virtual team leadership skills with the questionnaire shown in Table 3.4. A score of 5 represents full competence.

Which skill do you feel is most challenging for you as you lead virtual teams? Why? How can you improve your virtual skill set?

Case 3.1: IBM Socializes Its Virtual Teams

Around the world, virtual teams are on the rise. The virtual employee workforce includes road warriors who travel constantly, telecommuters who work from home, and people in one- or two-person offices spread out all over the globe. Collaborating with peers and team leaders separated by vast distances is made possible by technology, of course, but virtual managers are discovering that technology alone doesn't build teams.

A recent Aon Consulting report stated that using virtual teams can improve employee productivity. Additionally, a study of 80 global software teams indicated that well-managed virtual teams can actually outperform those in which members share office space.[32] Capitalizing on these advantages, IBM first began two decades ago to encourage its employees to engage in virtual team activity. Since that time, the company has been working on ways to build a sense of personal connection among its far-flung workers. "Humans are social animals. Without a real sense of community, most people just don't do their best work," says Dan Pelino, general manager of IBM's global public sector.[33]

Responding to the need for community among virtual team members, the company added a social networking site called SocialBlue. Employees post photos and bulletins about topics such as their kids, their dogs, their motorcycles, and what they did over the weekend. The social site has been a big hit with tens of thousands of IBM employees worldwide, from new entry-level hires to senior vice presidents. Employee surveys show that being able to work far from colleagues without losing touch has boosted employee satisfaction and makes top talent more inclined to stay with the company. IBM managers say SocialBlue has been a boon to teamwork and productivity—ironic, since the site recreates the kind of water-cooler chitchat that might once have been considered a waste of company time.

Case 3.2: Aon Hewitt Identifies Team Member Traits That Spell Success

Managers around the globe are grappling with ways to assemble successful virtual teams. Team composition that works well in face-to-face settings may not prove equally satisfactory when members are dispersed. Chad Thompson, senior consultant with Aon Hewitt, works to ensure that his virtual teams have what they need to work remotely. The technological part is fairly obvious: high-speed Internet connections, laptop computers, and virtual private network connectivity. The more challenging part lies in the soft skill set—how to select the right people for virtual teams.

Through his various projects as a benefits consultant, Thompson has learned that the best virtual workers tend to be those who thrive in interdependent work relationships. Contrary to popular thought, a person known as a loner tends not to perform well in a virtual team setting. Lone wolves typically lack communication and collaboration skills essential to virtual team work. "Interdependent work teams share common goals and responsibilities; at the same time, the team members are self-reliant and self-motivated," says Thompson. People who like regimented schedules and detailed instructions won't perform well in virtual settings either, as virtual work requires independent thought and a willingness to take initiative.[34]

According to Thompson, the most essential success trait for virtual team members is strong communication skills. Individuals must be able to draft easily read and understood messages that are to the point and unambiguous in meaning.[35]

Reflect

How do you rate yourself on the characteristics Thompson describes as key for virtual team members?

Apply

Prepare a slide presentation suitable for viewing by your company's staff that provides an overview of communication skills you feel are important for virtual team members to possess.

CHAPTER 4

Productive Virtual Team Meetings

While those who lead virtual meetings must perform all the same tasks required for effective face-to-face meetings, the technological component heightens the importance of preparation, leadership, and follow-up. Meeting participants might live in different time zones, speak different languages, and be uncomfortable with virtual interactions. Alternately, meeting participants might be in the same region or city but find virtual communication to be more efficient in terms of time and money.

In your virtual meetings, avoid trying to reproduce what happens in a face-to-face meeting. While the virtual meeting experience will differ from organization to organization, depending on the needs, resources, and intended meeting results, it will most certainly differ from face-to-face meetings that take place in the same organization.

Appropriate Technology Choices

Many different types of virtual meeting technology and software products are available, depending on the needs of your organization. Technology can provide a high-end telepresence experience at significant cost or more economical basic web conferencing. Choosing the most effective technology is not a simple process and is influenced by the organization's budget, the nature of the team task, and members' access to various technologies. Each organization must explore options and select the technology most suitable to its needs. We will not explore all available options nor make recommendations; rather, our primary purpose is to discuss a number of technology choices you might consider for your virtual meetings.

Telepresence Virtual Meetings

Some large organizations want a *telepresence experience* for participants; this technology creates the impression that people in different locations are actually in the same room. For example, Cisco's TelePresence is a system that uses ultra-high-definition life-size screens and lag-free voice over Internet protocol. Advanced features enhance the "high-intensity collaboration" capability needed for sophisticated planning sessions and problem resolution.[1] In this virtual boardroom, participants feel as if they are sitting across the table from someone a thousand miles away. As an alternative to purchasing such systems, however, many organizations desiring the telepresence experience are turning to their own in-house IT experts to find cost-effective alternatives that can deliver high-quality video and audio, natural eye contact and motion, life-size images, and intuitive operation. Such inside solutions allow companies to avoid major capital expenditures.

Web-Conferencing Options

Many organizations use web-conferencing software to set up virtual meetings. Such products are less expensive than the technology that provides a telepresence experience and are affordable for even small entities. Available products include the following:

- Cisco's WebEx is one of the oldest and most commonly used online meeting services and works well with Windows, Mac, smartphones, and tablets. Users receive high quality video and phone conferencing, screen sharing, and online collaboration tools, such as whiteboarding, note-taking, and annotations. Integration with other desktop applications such as Outlook makes it easy to schedule an appointment and add a meeting to it, e-mail the attendees quickly, and join a meeting on a mobile device.[2] The product starts at $49 per month for unlimited meetings and allows up to 25 participants per meeting.[3]
- Citrix's GoToMeeting integrates software such as Microsoft Office with features including videoconferencing, screen

sharing, chats, invitation options, meeting info, recording capability, drawing tools, and the ability to annotate shared content in real time.[4] The product is available for about $50 a month for up to 25 attendees and can be accessed from a Mac, PC, smartphone, or tablet.[5]

- MeetingBurner is a free online meeting service for up to 10 attendees. It has an easy-to-use interface, has fast load times, and includes Skype integration and screen sharing. Facilitators receive analytics that show how participants interact with the content.[6]
- Google+ Hangouts is another free service that has gained in popularity with the addition of screen sharing and document collaboration via Google Docs.[7]

Adobe Connect and iMeet are other examples of available conferencing services. New products are introduced each year, and the number likely will increase significantly as more businesses turn to virtual meetings as a means to save time and money.

Other Examples of Virtual Meeting Technology

Here are two additional options that may appeal to some organizations as they select virtual meeting solutions:

- IBM/Lotus offers virtual world meeting features through its product Sametime. These features include a virtual-reality meeting (similar to Second Life) with 3-D avatar attendees and presentation graphics displayed on a large movie-like screen. The virtual room is equipped with softphone voice communications and a whiteboard.[8]
- While not designed specifically for meetings, Skype is a free application that enables video and audio transmission and can compensate in part for a lack of face-to-face communication. The popular application bundles the capabilities of phone, traditional chat, and videoconferencing and works with Windows, Mac, and Linux operating systems.

Regardless of the collaboration tools used, the work of virtual teams can be enhanced by use of a dedicated website or intranet where information, data files, graphic materials, schedules, and reference collections can be stored and shared.

Meeting Preparation

An important question to ask before scheduling a virtual meeting is, "Should we meet?" You must determine if the purpose of the meeting is worth the time and cost of everyone's time. Answering the questions in Table 4.1 will help you answer the main one: Should we hold a virtual meeting?

If the meeting's purpose is to share information, then e-mails, file postings, and informal conversations might be just as effective as a meeting. However, if participants need to share opinions and knowledge and develop common thoughts, a meeting may be needed. In some cases, simply sharing information might be a legitimate reason to meet if spontaneous exchange is needed while everyone is together in real time. Knowing the desired end result defines the purpose of the meeting.

Additionally, the leader must decide the best time for the meeting, which may involve different time zones. For this reason, most virtual teams select a standing meeting time and stay with it for the duration of the project. Once the decision to meet has been made, preparation for the meeting can begin, following these steps.

Table 4.1 Should we hold a virtual meeting?

	Yes	No
Would e-mails or phone calls be as effective as a meeting?		
Is the input of participants needed, and will it be acted on?		
Does everyone have time to prepare for the meeting?		
Is enough information available to make the meeting productive?		
Can the desired end result be best achieved with a meeting?		

Identify the Meeting Objective

The meeting objective should be determined and communicated to those who will be in attendance. A productive meeting depends on clearly defined objectives that participants can work toward and against which progress can be measured. Rather than simply "discuss," the objective should be to "discuss and decide," or "discuss and plan," or "discuss and identify key barriers to success."[9] Following the meeting, participants need action steps and a plan, not simply a list of what happened in the last meeting.

Become Familiar with Meeting Elements

Conducting a virtual meeting takes preparation and special skills to ensure that everyone is engaged. An effective leader must demonstrate the skills discussed earlier, as well as comfort in leading a virtual meeting. If the leader or facilitator in charge of the meeting is not comfortable with the technology, a practice session may be necessary to ensure success. For example, in one business, a senior-level executive tried using a headset during a practice session and found that it was much easier to use his own speakerphone. If a practice walk-through is needed, use this time to test and make needed adjustments to the technology as well. The technology should facilitate, not overpower, the meeting's agenda.

Send an Advance Agenda

As with face-to-face meetings, virtual meeting agendas and supporting materials should be sent to participants 24 to 48 hours in advance. The more preparation work is done, the more likely the virtual meeting will be efficient. A sample agenda format is shown in Table 4.2.

If new members or guests will be participating in the meeting, they will benefit in particular from receiving in advance an overview of meeting attendance such as the one in Table 4.3.

The meeting should be planned to last for a reasonable length of time. If it must exceed 90 minutes or so, include short stretch breaks in the agenda.

Table 4.2 Sample meeting agenda

Meeting title:	Project update	
Date/Time:	Thursday, June 9, 10 a.m. (EDT)	
Meeting objective:	Assess progress on project and assign remaining tasks	
	Topic	**Speaker**
8:30–8:45	Progress since last meeting	Team leader and members
8:45–9:00	Update on manufacturing issues	Production manager; member discussion
9:00–9:15	Discussion of adjusted delivery timeline	Team leader and members
9:15–9:30	Recap and wrap up; individual member assignments	Facilitator; member input

Table 4.3 Meeting attendance overview

Invited participants	Attending	Not attending
Name—Represented area		
Name—Represented area		
Name—Represented area		
Name—Represented area		
Name—Represented area		

Facilitation of Effective Online Meetings

Virtual meetings have unique challenges that must be anticipated and addressed by the leader. The following actions increase the likelihood of a smooth, productive meeting.

Assure a Smooth Start

The meeting should start at the time announced in advance, so participants should assemble themselves slightly ahead of the announced starting time to gather materials and check connections. Starting late costs the organization money and wastes the time of participants. At the start of the meeting, all participants should introduce themselves by name so everyone knows who is in attendance and has a sense of the group composition and locations. Following introductions, the leader or meeting facilitator should review where the group is with their progress and refer to the meeting agenda.

Appoint a Facilitator

In addition to the team leader, a *moderator* or *facilitator* may be appointed to help the meeting move along. This person can keep track of the participants who are waiting to speak and assist with technical aspects of the meeting if needed. The leader can then focus on the meeting purpose and objectives. For some organizations, a designated support person may be assigned to monitor all aspects of the technology. Other roles may be assigned as needed, including a recordkeeper to prepare official meeting minutes and provide follow-up communication to all participants. For meetings where most of the participants are in one room, the facilitator might tie a balloon on the phone or webcam to remind team members of the remote participants.[10]

Control Speaking

Spoken words should be carefully chosen. If participants are connected only by audio, they will not understand if the leader points to a line item and says, "Let's talk about this." Questions and comments should be repeated if there is a chance that some cannot hear all speakers. Sometimes a problem occurs when participants try to talk over one another. However, software products typically include a feature allowing participants to click a particular key on their keyboards to signal that they want to talk. The leader or facilitator can then recognize participants in turn.

Seek Consensus Frequently

Frequent summaries of what has been discussed and decided help ensure that everyone is on board with the meeting's progress. Roll-call voting should be conducted for important decisions. *Polling* is a typical technological feature the leader can use to have participants respond to questions presented in true or false, yes or no, or multiple-choice formats. Results can be instantly displayed for all participants.

Keep Everyone on Task

As with all meetings, virtual meeting participants must not be allowed to get sidetracked. Keeping participants engaged in a virtual meeting is particularly challenging, as people can easily "multitask" by reading something else, checking e-mail, or moving about for food or drink. If some participants are obviously not participating or responding, the leader or facilitator may need to single them out for response to encourage them to rejoin the meeting. However, the more engaging and focused the meeting, the less likely participants will lose interest.

Evaluate Meeting Effectiveness

A meeting evaluation should be completed at the end of each meeting. Items to evaluate should include the overall focus on the issues, efficiency regarding time and discussion of issues, participation, and results. The leader may schedule a few minutes at the end of the meeting to ask for feedback from participants on the meeting effectiveness. This activity provides useful input for planning future meetings and also encourages involvement and collaboration from meeting participants.

Meeting Follow-Up

Meeting follow-up actually is more easily achieved in virtual settings than face-to-face because of the permanent archive of communication exchanges afforded by electronic environments. Notes and recordings from the meeting should be converted to meeting minutes and made available to all participants within two days of the meeting. Minutes from all meetings should follow a consistent format and include a "Decisions Made" section to highlight actions. A sample template for meeting minutes is shown in Table 4.4. Other templates are available at the Microsoft Office Online website: http://office.microsoft.com/en-us/templates/ct10 1172601033.aspx.

Minutes and related documents can be e-mailed or posted to a common space where they can be reviewed and referred to later as needed by the various team members.

Table 4.4 Meeting minutes template

Subject:	
Leader:	
Facilitator:	
Location:	
Date/Time:	
Attendees:	

Key points discussed

No.	Topic	Highlights
1		
2		
3		

Decisions made

1	
2	
3	

Agreed upon actions

No.	Action item	Person responsible
1		
2		
3		

Case 4.1: Lullabot Employees Share Insights for Virtual Workers

Lullabot, formed in 2006, is a 100 percent distributed company with no central office. According to Jeff Robbins, the company's cofounder and CEO, while all of Lullabot's employees work virtually from home or a distant location, they are not remote workers because they stay well connected.[11] In a distributed organization, both communication and culture must adapt to accommodate for the lack of a centralized workplace. Lullabot's intercontinental work team offers the following list of highly effective habits for virtual workers:[12]

- Get dressed as if you are going to work. Productivity is boosted when you shower, dress, and report for your workday. While dress may be a bit more casual, readying yourself for a purpose helps you get in focused work mode.
- Have a schedule. A distinct advantage of virtual work is being able to find your own ideal schedule and pattern for productivity. No matter how off-beat your schedule may be, sticking to the pattern helps you use time effectively and avoid working all the time with reduced productivity.
- Have a dedicated workspace. Keep organized, and do what you can to differentiate work and leisure.
- Get out. Just as leaving a physically located job for lunch can help you rejuvenate, the same is true for leaving your home workspace. Run an errand, exercise, or at least retreat for a while from the computer.
- Connect. Create situations for face-to-face time with clients or colleagues using videochat via Skype, Google Hangouts, or GoToMeeting rather than sending an e-mail. Take part in meetings and gatherings of a professional organization or group in your area.

Lullabot personnel remind other virtual workers that there is no single right or wrong way to work from home. They encourage virtual workers to try various strategies to find their own best practices.

Reflect

What other highly effective habits of distributed workers would you add to the list developed by Lullabot personnel?

Apply

Interview one or more virtual workers to learn more about the advantages and challenges of their work arrangement. Prepare an oral presentation with appropriate visuals to share your findings.

Case 4.2: Accenture Keeps Its Virtual Workforce Connected

Accenture, a multinational and widely distributed consulting firm, has offices located around the globe. With thousands of global employees working mostly at client sites in more than 100 companies, Accenture must focus continually on keeping its virtual workforce connected with one another and with the company.[13]

Accenture has made 13 consecutive appearances on Fortune's "World's Most Admired Companies" list and has been recognized with various awards that recognize its strides in diversity and employee development. Completing an extensive "new joiner" orientation program is a requirement of every new consultant hired at Accenture. Following orientation, each new hire is assigned a career counselor to help identify career paths and navigate various work-related obstacles. Each time an employee is promoted, more training is provided, with the average Accenture employee spending about 75 hours in training each year. Managers receive specific training in leading virtual teams, including topics such as how to be sensitive to time zone issues and how to encourage initial chitchat in online exchanges.

A variety of technology tools assists Accenture in keeping its employees connected. Cisco's TelePresence web-conferencing platform facilitates communication, and the company also has a People Pages site (the company's version of Facebook), which allows employees to read personal profiles and send messages to each other. The Careers Marketplace website provides employees with information about careers with Accenture and links them to open positions. Keeping more than 300,000 worldwide employees connected is no small task, but Accenture's management works concertedly to make sure it happens.[14]

Reflect

What additional technical and nontechnical strategies could be employed to promote connectedness among virtual team members?

Apply

Develop a handbook for "new joiner" orientation to help people assimilate effectively into virtual teams. Your handbook, suitable for posting electronically, should include guidelines, tips, resources, and other useful information.

Summary

Virtual teams continue to grow in popularity because of the advantages they offer to geographically dispersed organizations. Most teams operate virtually at least some of the time as members exploit available technologies to supplement and at times take the place of face-to-face meetings.

In the global business environment, the success of many organizations depends on the effective functioning of intercultural virtual teams. Other aspects of diversity further complicate the effective functioning of virtual teams. Team selection is crucial to project success, and training for the virtual experience greatly increases the chance of success. Individuals possessing the specific skill set needed for success in virtual teams are highly marketable in a wide variety of organizations. Virtual teams whose members recognize, respect, and respond to differing behavioral expectations enhance their prospects for achieving high performance levels. Education about the dynamics of virtual teams serves to enhance team member commitment and raise the probability for team success.

Leadership of virtual teams requires a special skill set that differs somewhat from that required in more traditional settings. While virtual teams face various challenges not encountered by face-to-face teams, various strategies can be applied to make the virtual team experience a successful and satisfying one for participants. Selection of technology is key to virtual team functioning and should be determined based on the goals and activities of the team. As with any meeting, a virtual meeting must be well planned, well managed, and well documented.

The world is truly becoming smaller, and virtual teams are an essential element in global activity. Time spent developing virtual team skills in yourself and others and mastering virtual meetings is well invested and will pay dividends in higher productivity, greater job satisfaction, and richer relationships with colleagues around the world.

Notes

Chapter 1

1. Leonhard (1995).
2. Minton-Eversole (2012, July 19).
3. Narisi (2011, June 29).
4. Minton-Eversole (2012, July 19).
5. Turmel (2010).
6. Step up search for talent in digital age (2007, June).
7. Berry (2011).
8. iPass Inc (2014).
9. Conlin (2009, July 16).
10. Hunt (1993).
11. AppendTo (2015).
12. Reynolds (2014).
13. King (2008, May 19).

Chapter 2

1. VanBroekhoven (2012, June 18).
2. Matthews (2015, May 11).
3. Bruzzese (2013, October 20).
4. Lehman and DuFrene (2011).
5. Lancaster and Stillman (2002).
6. Turmel (2010, July 5).
7. Helgesen and Johnson (2010).
8. Lawlor (2006).
9. Tuckman (1965).
10. Dunkel and Meierewert (2004).
11. Hawkrigg (2007, March 12).
12. Neyer and Harzing (2008).
13. Dunkel and Meierewert (2004).
14. Hurn and Jenkins (2000).
15. Neyer and Harzing (2008).
16. Collaborative teams (2008, June).
17. Neyer and Harzing (2008).
18. Nawati and Craig (2006, March).
19. Neyer and Harzing (2008).

20. Maznevski and Peterson (1997).
21. Kirkman et al. (2002), p. 69.
22. Dunkel and Meierewert (2004); Hurn and Jenkins (2000); Nawati and Craig (2006, March).
23. Tuckman and Jensen (1977).
24. Kirkman et al. (2002), p. 69.
25. Foster (2015).
26. Foster (2015).

Chapter 3

1. Hawkrigg (2007, March 12).
2. Dargin (2015).
3. DuFrene and Lehman (2011).
4. Gratton and Erickson (2007, November).
5. Gratton and Erickson (2007, November).
6. Ferrazzi (2012, October 24).
7. Conlin (2008, January 31).
8. Fisher (2009, November 20).
9. Adler and Gundersen (2007); Hurn and Jenkins (2000).
10. Watkins (2013, June 27).
11. Grenny (2010, January).
12. Ozimek (2013, January 6).
13. Jarvenpaa and Leidner (1999).
14. Naish (2009, October).
15. Naish (2009, October).
16. Dargin (2015).
17. Fjermestad (2009, March).
18. King (2008, May 19).
19. Dargin (2015).
20. Watkins (2013, June 27).
21. Mortensen and O'Leary (2012, April 16).
22. Stillman (2012, June 5).
23. Patterson (2008, July 9).
24. Turmel (2010).
25. Mortensen and O'Leary (2012, April 16).
26. Trapani (2009, June 16).
27. Hanke (2009, June 16).
28. Lehman and DuFrene (2016).
29. Patterson (2008, July 9).
30. Watkins (2013, June 27).

31. Knight (2015, February 10).
32. Knight (2015, February 10).
33. Ferrazzi (2014).
34. Fisher (2009, November 20).
35. Leonard (2011).
36. Leonard (2011).

Chapter 4

1. Perez (2012, March 27).
2. Henry (2012, January 22).
3. WebEx (2015).
4. Online meetings get better: GoToMeeting 3.0 (2007).
5. GoToMeeting (2015).
6. Fance (2012).
7. Henry (2012, January 22).
8. Fontana (2008, January 23).
9. Krattenmaker (2008, February 27).
10. White (2014).
11. Robbins (2014, May 22).
12. Lee (2013, March).
13. Accenture (2015).
14. Marquez (2008, September 22).

References

Accenture. (2015). Accenture website. Retrieved from https://www.accenture.com/us-en/company#

Adler, N. J., & Gundersen, A. (2007). *International dimensions of organizational behavior*. Mason, OH: Thomson South-Western.

AppendTo. (2015). About appendTo. Retrieved from http://appendto.com

Berry, G. R. (2011). Enhancing effectiveness in virtual teams. *Journal of Business Communication, 48*(2), 186–206.

Bruzzese, A. (2013, October 20). On the job: New generation is arriving in the workplace. *USA Today*. Retrieved from http://www.usatoday.com/story/money/columnist/bruzzese/2013/10/20/on-the-job-generation-z/2999689/

Collaborative teams. (2008, June). *Bulletpoint, 152*, 3–5.

Conlin, M. (2009, June 16). Is there a virtual worker personality? *BusinessWeek Online*. Retrieved from http://www.bloomberg.com/bw/stories/2009-06-16/is-there-a-virtual-worker-personality-businessweek-business-news-stock-market-and-financial-advice

Conlin, M. (2008, January 31). Working remotely . . . or remotely working? Part two. *Bloomsberg Businessweek*. Retrieved from http://www.businessweek.com/careers/managementiq/archives/2008/01/working_remotel_1.html

Dargin, S. (2015). Top 6 best practices for managing virtual teams. Corporate Education Group. Retrieved from http://www.corpedgroup.com/resources/pm/6BestPracticesMVT.asp

DuFrene, D. D., & Lehman, C. M. (2011). *Building high-performance teams*. Mason, OH: South-Western/Cengage Learning.

Dunkel, A., & Meierewert, S. (2004). Cultural standards and their impact on teamwork: An empirical analysis of Austrian, German, Hungarian and Spanish culture differences. *Journal for East European Management Studies, 9*, 147–174.

Fance, C. (2012). Online meeting and web conferencing tools—best of. *Hongkiat*. Retrieved from http://www.hongkiat.com/blog/online-meeting-tools/

Ferrazzi, K. (2014, December). Getting virtual teams right. *Harvard Business Review*. Retrieved from https://hbr.org/2014/12/getting-virtual-teams-right

Ferrazzi, K. (2012, October 24). How successful virtual teams collaborate. *Harvard Business Review*. Retrieved from https://hbr.org/2012/10/how-to-collaborate-in-a-virtua/

Fisher, A. (2009, December 10). How to build a (strong) virtual team: In a world where fewer and fewer employees work in the same location as their bosses,

IBM is figuring out how to bring together far-flung coworkers. *Fortune*. Retrieved from http://archive.fortune.com/2009/11/16/news/companies/ibm_virtual_manager.fortune/index.htm

Fjermestad, J. (2009, March). In practice: Communication activities of high- and low-performing teams. *Chief Learning Officer, 8*(3), 36–39.

Fontana, J. (2008, January 23). Lotus toying with Sametime features including virtual world meetings. *Network World*. Retrieved from http://www.networkworld.com/article/2282565/software/lotus-toying-with-sametime-features-including-virtual-world-meetings.html

Foster, W. (2015). How to build culture in a remote team. *Zapier*. Retrieved from https://zapier.com/learn/the-ultimate-guide-to-remote-working/how-build-culture-remote-team/

GoToMeeting. (2015). Plans and pricing. Retrieved from https://www.gotomeeting.com/meeting/pricing?c_name=becauselpvar2

Gratton, L., & Erickson, T. (2007, November). Ways to build collaborative teams. *Harvard Business Review*, 101–109.

Grenny, J. (2010, January). Virtual teamwork. *Leadership Excellence*, 17.

Hanke, S. (2009, June 16). How to create e-mails that generate action. *Business-WeekOnline*, 21. Retrieved from http://www.bloomberg.com/bw/stories/2009-06-16/how-to-create-e-mails-that-generateactionbusinessweek-business-news-stock-market-and-financial-advice

Hawkrigg, J. (2007, March 12). Virtual teams need human touch. *Canadian HR Reporter, 20*(5), 16.

Helgesen, S., & Johnson, J. (2010). *The female vision: Women's real power at work*. San Francisco, CA: Berrett-Koehler.

Henry, A. (2012, January 22). Five best online meeting services. *Lifehacker*. Retrieved from http://lifehacker.com/5878067/five-best-online-meeting-services

Hunt, V. D. (1993). *Managing for quality: Integrating quality and business strategy*. Homewood, IL: Business One Irwin.

Hurn, B. F., & Jenkins, M. (2000). International peer group development. *Industrial and Commercial Training, 32*(4), 128–131.

iPass Inc. (2014). The iPass mobile enterprisee report. Retrieved from http://moreinfo.ipass.com/mobile-enterprise-report.html

Jarvenpaa, S. L., & Leidner, D. E. (1999). Communication and trust in global virtual teams. Special Issue: Communication Processes for Virtual Organizations. *Organization Science, 10*(6), 791–815.

King, R. (2008, May 19). How virtual teams succeed. *BusinessWeekOnline*, 27.

Kirkman, B. L., Benson, R., Gibson, C. B., Tesluk, P. E., & McPherson, S. O. (2002). Five challenges to virtual team success: Lessons from Sabre, Inc. *Academy of Management Executive, 16*(3), 67–79.

Knight, R. (2015, February 10). How to manage remote direct reports. *Harvard Business Review*. Retrieved from https://hbr.org/2015/02/how-to-manage-remote-direct-reports

Krattenmaker, T. (2008, February 27). Make every meeting matter. Harvard Management Update. *Harvard Business Review*. Retrieved from https://hbr.org/2008/02/make-every-meeting-matter/

Lancaster, L. C., & Stillman, D. (2002). *When generations collide*. New York, NY: HarperCollins.

Lawlor, C. (2006). Gender interactions in computer-mediated computer conferencing. *The Journal of Distance Education, 21*(2). Retrieved from http://eric.ed.gov/?id=EJ807802

Lee, E. (2013, March). How working at home works (for us). Retrieved from https://www.lullabot.com/blog/article/how-working-home-works-us

Lehman, C. M., & DuFrene, D. D. (2016). *BCOM7*. Boston. Cengage Learning.

Leonard, B. (2011, June 1). Managing virtual teams. *Society for Human Resource Management. HR Magazine*. Retrieved from http://www.madisonpg.com/wp-content/uploads/2011/06/HR-Magazine-Managing-Virtual-Teams.pdf

Leonhard, W. (1995). *The underground guide to telecommuting: Slightly askew advice on leaving the rat race behind*. Reading, MA: Addison Wesley.

Marquez, J. (2008, September 22). Connecting a virtual workforce. *Workforce Management*, 1–25.

Matthews, C. (2015, May 11). Millennials have taken over the American workforce. *Fortune*. Retrieved from http://fortune.com/2015/05/11/millennials-have-taken-over-the-american-workforce/

Maznevski, M. L., & Peterson, M. F. (1997). Societal values, social interpretation, and multinational teams. In C. Granrose (Ed.), *Cross-cultural work groups* (pp. 61–89). Thousand Oaks, CA: Sage.

Minton-Eversole, T. (2012, July 19). Virtual teams used most by global organizations, survey says. *Society for Human Resource Management*. Retrieved from http://www.shrm.org/hrdisciplines/orgempdev/articles/pages/virtual-teamsusedmostbyglobalorganizations,surveysays.aspx

Mortensen, M., & O'Leary, M. (2012, April 16). Managing a virtual team. *Harvard Business Review*. Retrieved from http://bundlr.com/clips/51eb25eaa6c04511ed00091d

Naish, R. (2009, October). Take the virtual lead. *e.learning age*, 10.

Narisi, S. (2011, June 29). Most employees work remotely—Can your department support them? *ITmanagerdaily.com*. Retrieved from http://www.itmanagerdaily.com/most-employees-working-remotely-can-your-department-support-them/

Nawati, D. A., & Craig, A. (2006, March). Behavioral adaptation within cross-cultural virtual teams. *IEEE Transactions, 49*(1), 44–56.

Neyer, A., & Harzing, A. (2008). The impact of culture on interactions: Five lessons learned from the European Commission. *European Management Journal, 26*(5), 325–334.

Online meetings get better: GoToMeeting 3.0. (2007, August 21). *PC Magazine,* 43.

Ozimek, R. (2013, January 6). Four strategies to increase virtual team happiness and productivity. *PICnetblog.* Retrieved from http://blog.picnet. net/2013/01/06/four-strategies-to-increase-virtual-team-happiness-and-productivity/

Patterson, K. (2008, July 9). Crucial conversations over the phone. *Crucial Skills, 6*(28). Retrieved from http://www.vitalsmarts.com/userfiles/File/newsletter/ Newsletter%20070908QA.htm

Perez, J. C. (2012, March 27). Cisco boosts telepresence system with new collaboration features. *PCWorld.* Retrieved from http://www.pcworld.com/ article/252642/cisco_boosts_telepresence_system_with_new_collaboration_ features.html

Reynolds, B. W. (2015, March 30). 76 virtual companies and distributed teams. Retrieved from https://www.flexjobs.com/blog/post/76-virtual-companies-and-distributed-teams/

Reynolds, B. W. (2014, March 14). 26 virtual companies that thrive on remote work. *Flexjobs.* Retrieved from http://www.flexjobs.com/blog/post/25-virtual-companies-that-thrive-on-remote-work/

Robbins, J. (2014, May 22). What is a distributed company? *Business.* Retrieved from https://www.lullabot.com/articles/what-is-a-distributed-company

Step up search for talent in digital age. (2007, June). *Accountancy Ireland,* 98.

Stillman, J. (2012, June 5). Remote work study: Distance makes the heart grow fonder. *GIGAOM.* Retrieved from https://gigaom.com/2012/06/05/remote-work-study-distance-makes-the-heart-grow-fonder/

Trapani, G. (2009, June 16). Master the art of working remotely. *HBR Blog Network.* Retrieved from http://blogs.hbr.org/trapani/2009/06/master-the-art-of-working-with.html

Tuckman, B. W. (1965). Developmental sequence in small groups. *Psychological Bulletin, 63,* 384–399.

Tuckman, B. W., & Jensen, M. A. C. (1977). Stages of small group development revisited. *Group and Organizational Studies, 2,* 419–427.

Turmel, W. (2010). Three reasons why virtual teams fail and how to see it coming. Great Web Meetings White Paper. Retrieved from https://www. thecorporatetoolbox.com/system/media_files/files/59/original_3%20 Reasons%20Virtual%20Teams%20Fail%20%20And%20How%20to%20 See%20It%20Coming%20by%20Wayne%20Turmel.pdf

Turmel, W. (2010, July 5). Telecommuting: Why men and women work differently? *bnet.com*. Retrieved from http://www.bnet.com/blog/virtual-manager/telecommuting-why-men-and-women-work-differently/411

VanBroekhoven, J. (2012, June 18). The generational workforce of the future. *Hogan Assessments*. Retrieved from http://info.hoganassessments.com/blog/bid/171186/The-Generational-Workforce-of-the-Future

Vencat, E. F. (2006, December 3). Communication: Virtual meeting. *Newsweek International*. Retrieved from http://www.newsweek.com/communication-virtual-meeting-105157

Watkins, M. (2013, June 27). Making virtual teams work: Ten basic principles. *Harvard Business Review*. Retrieved from https://hbr.org/2013/06/making-virtual-teams-work-ten/

WebEx. (2015). WebEx meetings pricing. Retrieved from http://www.webex.com/pricing/

White, M. (2014). The management of virtual teams and virtual meetings. *Business Information Review, 31*(2), 111–117. doi:10.1177/0266382114540979

Index

Note: Page numbers with *f* indicate figures; those with *t* indicate tables.

Accenture, 59–60

Adobe Connect, 51

Adjourning stage, 21

Advantages of virtual teams, 3–4
  in cost savings, 3–4
  in decision making, 4
  in employer/employee efficiencies, 4
  in facility and environmental
    benefits, 4
  in labor pool enhancement, 4

age diversity, 11–14
  Baby Boomers (or Boomers), 12
  generational competence and,
    13–14
  Generation Xers, 12
  Generation Z, 12–13
  Matures (or seniors over 65), 11–12
  Millennials (Generation Yers), 12
  stereotyping according to age and,
    14

Aon Hewitt, 47

AppendTo, 7–9

Asians, 16, 18, 42

asynchronous communications, 3,
  5, 38

asynchronous exchanges, 3

Austrians, 18

Baby Boomers (or Boomers), 12

behavior, four Cs, 6
  commitment, 6
  communication, 6
  contribution, 6
  cooperation, 6

British, 17, 19

challenges of virtual teams, 4–7
  See also diversity challenges
  in behaviors, 6–7
  in cohesion, 5–6
  in coordination, 7

cultural complications, 6
  in isolation, 5
  in leadership, 7
  in nonverbal cues, 5

Cisco
  People Pages, 59
  TelePresence, 59
  WebEx, 50

Citrix, 50–51

code of conduct, 36–37

cohesion, 5–6
  collaboration, 28
  executive support and, 28
  HR practices and, 29
  team formation/structure and, 29
  team leaders and, 29

commitment, in four Cs of behavior,
  6

communication. *See under* challenges
  of virtual teams; *see* face-to-face
    interactions; technology-
    mediated communication
  in four Cs of behavior, 6

computer-mediated communication
  (CMC), 15

concentration, gender differences in,
  14

conflict. *See* diversity challenges
  contribution, in four Cs of
    behavior, 6
  cooperation, in four Cs of behavior,
    6

coordination, lack of, 6

cost savings, 3–4

cross-cultural awareness, 20

cross-cultural training, 20

*Crucial Conversations: Tools for
  Talking when Stakes Are High*
  (Patterson), 38

cultural differences, 10, 15–21
  conflict and, 18

consideration and, 20
cross-cultural awareness and, 20
cross-cultural training and, 20
groupthink and, 19
harmony and, 21
language training and, 20
leadership styles and, 18
overcoming (Johnson & Johnson
    case), 9–10
politeness and, 18
stages of team development and,
    16–17
stereotypes and, 20
women and, status of, 18

decision making, 4
different time, different place
    interactions, 2–3
    different time, same place
        interactions, 3
diversity challenges, 11–24. *See also*
        cultural differences
    age differences, 11–14
    gender differences, 14–15
    stages of team development and,
        16–17, 16*f*
    virtual team culture at Zapier,
        23–24
documentation, 41–42

electronic communications. *See*
        technology-mediated
        communication
    email, 39
    creating, 39–40
    emoticons in, 38
    etiquette, 39
technology options, 38emoticons, 38
employer/employee efficiencies, 4
environmental benefits, 4

Facebook, 29, 51
face-to-face interactions
    benefits of, 32
    communication styles and, 14
    gender differences in, 14–15
    degree of "virtuality" in, 2

in first-year team strategies, 32
in team member preparation,
    31–33
tone, delivery, and body language
    in, 40
vs. virtual interactions, 49
facility benefits, 4
*Female Vision: Women's Real Power
    at Work, The* (Helgesen and
    Johnson), 14
first-year team strategies, 25–26
    communication strategies in, 26
    face-to-face meetings in, 25
    performance monitoring in, 26
    task accountability in, 26
    team roles in, 25–26
focus, gender differences in, 14–15
forming stage, 16–17,16*f*
Foster, W., 23

gender differences, 14–15
    in communication styles, 15
    in focus and concentration, 14
    in thinking, 14
generational competence, 13–14
Generation Xers, 12
Generation Yers (or Millennials), 12
Generation Z, 12–13
Germans, 16, 18
Google Docs, 51
Google Hangouts, 23, 51, 58
GoToMeeting (Citrix), 23, 50–51
groupthink, 19

harmony, cultural, 21
Helgesen, S., 14
Hewlett-Packard, 30
HR practices, 29

IBM, 45–46, 51
iMeet, 51
instant messaging, 15, 37
interactions, types of, 2–3
intercultural training, 42–43
isolation, 5
Italians, 19

Japanese, 17, 19
Jenson, M. A, 21
Johnson, J., 14
Johnson & Johnson, 9–10, 36

labor pool enhancement, 4
language barriers, 15
language training, 20
Latin Americans, 16, 20
leadership. *See* team leadership
Leonhard, W., 1
Lotus, 51
Lullabot employees, 57–58

maintenance goal, 5
Matures (or seniors over 65), 11–12
Meeting Burner, 51
meeting follow-up, 56–57
meeting minutes, 56–57
meetings. *See* virtual meetings
Microsoft Office, 50, 56
Millennials (or Generation Yers), 12
monochronic cultures, 18
mutual understanding, 20

nonverbal cues, 5
norming stage, 16*f,* 18–19

Patterson, K., 38
Pelino, D., 46
PeoplePages (Cisco), 59
performance monitoring, 26
performing stage, *16f, 19–21*
phone calls, 40–41
Portuguese, 19
progress assessment, 44

questions, encouraging use of, 21

remote communications. *See*
    technology-mediated
    communication
Robbins, J., 49

Sabre, Inc., 21–23
Sametime (IBM/Lotus), 51
same time, different place
    interactions, 2–3

same time, same place interactions, 2
Skype (Microsoft), 51
Slack, 23
SocialBlue (IBM), 46
socializing virtual teams (IBM case),
    45–46
social networking, 33, 46
software products. *See* technology and
    software products
Sorensen, Karan, 9, 36
Spaniards, 17
stages of team development, 16–17,
    16*f*
    adjourning stage, 21
    forming stage, 16–17
    norming stage, 18–19
    performing stage, 19–21
    storming stage, 17–18
stereotyping
    according to age, 14
    overcoming, 20
storming stage, 17–18
swift trust paradigm principle, 33–34
synchronous communications, 2, 5,
    38

task accountability
    in facilitation of meetings, 56
    in first-year team strategies, 26
task goal, 5
team accomplishments, recognition
    of, 44–45
team cohesion, 25, 33, 34
team development
    cultural differences in, 15–21
    personal characteristics to promote, 1
    stages of, 16–17
team leadership
    assessment of, 27–28*t*, 45
    for cultural harmony, 21
    ineffective, 7
    selection of, 26–29
    styles, in storming stage, 18
team meeting assessment, 42–44
    instrument for, *42, 43t*
    Virtual Team Progress Assessment
        exercise in, 42, 44
team member assessment, 30–31*t*
team member preparation, 31–33

face-to-face time in, 32
team scope and purpose in, 32
technological competence in, 32
virtual presence in, 32–33
team membership, 29–31
team roles in first-year team strategies,
    25–26
team strategies, 25–48
    documentation, 41–42
    first-year, 25–26
    intercultural training, 42–43
    leadership selection, 26, 28–29
    team accomplishments, recognition
        of, 44–45
    team assessment, 42–44
    team member preparation, 31–33
    team membership, 29–31
    trust building, 33–34
technology and software products,
    51–52
    for effective, 37–38
    Sametime (IBM/Lotus), 51
    Skype (Microsoft), 51
    TelePresence (Cisco), 59
    for telepresence virtual meetings, 50
    for web-conferencing, 50–51
technology-mediated communication
    code of conduct for, 36–37
    collaborative skills and, 28
    cultural and psychological hurdles
        of, 10
    effective, 35–41
    electronic meetings and, 15
    e-mail and, 37–39
    in first-year team strategies, 25–26
    open and rich, 34
    phone calls and, 40–41
    practices, studies of, 29
    rules of engagement in, 10, 36
    schedule of contact for, 37
    technology-mediated, 1, 32
    trust and, 33–34
TelePresence (Cisco), 50
telepresence virtual meetings, 50
thinking, gender differences in, 14
Thompson, C., 47, 48
training
    cross-cultural, 20
    intercultural, 42–43

language, 20
transparency, 21
trust, 33–34
    collaboration and, 28–29
    communication and, 34–41
    grounds for, 34
    swift trust paradigm principle and,
        33–34
    team cohesion and, 33, 34
Tuckman, B., 15, 21
Twitter, 33

Underground Guide to Telecommuting,
    The (Leonhard), 1

videoconferencing, 1, 22, 25, 27, 30,
    37, 50, 51
Virtual Meeting Evaluation, 43t
virtual meetings, 49–60
    meeting follow-up, 56–57
    technology and software productsin,
        51–52
    virtual meetings, facilitation of,
        54–56
    consensus, seeking frequently, 55
    keeping everyone on task, 56
    meeting evaluation, 56
    moderator or facilitator,
        appointing, 55
    speaking, control of, 55
    starting, 54–55
virtual meetings, preparation for,
    52–54
    decision to meet and, 52, 52t
    elements of meeting, becoming
        familiar with, 53
    meeting agendas, sending, 53–54t
    meeting attendance, overview of,
        53, 54t
    objective of meeting, identifying,
        53
    virtual presence, 32–33
Virtual Team Leadership Skills
    Assessment, 45
Virtual Team Progress Assessment
    exercise, 42, 44
virtual teams
    advantages of, 3–4
    challenges of, 4–7

degree of "virtuality" in, 2
diversity challenges in, 11–24
interactions in, types of, 2–3
meeting assessments in, 43
meetings, productive, 49–60
personal characteristics to promote
    development of, 1
popularity of, 1–10
role of, in global business
    environment, 1
size of, 3
strategies for success, 1, 25–48
terms for, 1

trend toward, 1
trust in, building, 21–23
virtual meetings and, 49–59

webcams, 5
web-conferencing software, 50–51, 59
WebEx, 50
When Generations Collide (Lancaster
    and Stillman), 13
women, cross-cultural differences in
    status of, 18

Zapier, 23–24

OTHER TITLES IN OUR CORPORATE COMMUNICATION COLLECTION

Debbie DuFrene, Stephen F. Austin State University, Editor

- *Managerial Communication: Evaluating the Right Dose* by J. David Johnson
- *Web Content: A Writer's Guide* by Janet Mizrahi
- *Intercultural Communication for Managers* by Michael B. Goodman
- *Persuasive Business Presentations: Using the Problem-Solution Method to Influence Decision Makers to Take Action* by Gary May
- *SPeak Performance: Using the Power of Metaphors to Communicate Vision, Motivate People, and Lead Your Organization to Success* by Jim Walz
- *Today's Business Communication: A How-To Guide for the Modern Professional* by Jason L. Snyder and Robert Forbus
- *Leadership Talk: A Discourse Approach to Leader Emergence* by Robyn Walker and Jolanta Aritz
- *Communication Beyond Boundaries* by Payal Mehra
- *Managerial Communication* by Reginald L. Bell and Jeanette S. Martin
- *Writing for the Workplace: Business Communication for Professionals* by Janet Mizrahi
- *Get Along, Get It Done, Get Ahead: Interpersonal Communication in the Diverse Workplace* by Geraldine E. Hynes

Announcing the Business Expert Press Digital Library

Concise e-books business students need for classroom and research

This book can also be purchased in an e-book collection by your library as

- a one-time purchase,
- that is owned forever,
- allows for simultaneous readers,
- has no restrictions on printing, and
- can be downloaded as PDFs from within the library community.

Our digital library collections are a great solution to beat the rising cost of textbooks. E-books can be loaded into their course management systems or onto students' e-book readers.
The **Business Expert Press** digital libraries are very affordable, with no obligation to buy in future years. For more information, please visit **www.businessexpertpress.com/librarians**. To set up a trial in the United States, please email **sales@businessexpertpress.com**.